Modern Bemba

A concise introduction to the Bemba language

kasahorow

Everyone is an African

Revised 2022-07-28

© 2011

KWID: G-KKK25-BEM-EN-2022-07-28

Nana Akua, Kwesi Kwaa Prah

Contents

Preface

kasahorow loves Cisungu

Our mission is to teach inclusion.

The first step to inclusive Cisungu usage is to write Cisungu with consistent spelling rules. If you and I use the same spelling, we understand each other better.

Consistent spelling may be pronounced in different ways in different places. In other words, the spelling of an inclusive Cisungu word does not indicate how to pronounce it. In fact, we believe there is no such thing as correct pronunciation. Rather, we think your pronunciation is correct when you can be understood by other Cisungu speakers.

Sign up to receive updates in your Cisungu at `https://bem.kasahorow.org/subscribe`.

Sharing License

You may freely photocopy and redistribute this book for private or commercial use. No restrictions. Yes go ahead. Do good by sharing.

Errata

All mistakes are ours. When you find one, please let us know so we can fix it.

Please send corrections to help@kasahorow.org.

Modern Cisungu

Modern Cisungu is a written form of Cisungu. It is faster to read. It is also faster to understand. This is because Modern Cisungu has been simplified in the following ways:

1. Modern Cisungu uses the plain alphabet of Cisungu.

2. Modern Cisungu uses only basic word classes: nouns, verbs, and conjunctions.

3. Modern Cisungu uses unique spellings for distinct meanings.

4. Modern Cisungu uses spaces between distinct words in a dictionary.

5. Modern Cisungu uses the active voice only.

This guide is designed to get you up to speed quickly with the Modern Cisungu language. We hope that after getting through it you will be able to read, write and speak basic Cisungu sentences to express the following range of concepts:

1. muntu musuma [good person]

2. Ine ndatemwa Efia. [I love Efia.]

3. Kofi alyile ichakulya. [Kofi ate the food.]

4. Mailo, Amina akaisa ng'anda. [Tomorrow, Amina will come home.]

5. Mulumendo na mukashana balafwaya ichakulya. [The boy and the girl want food.]

For teachers of Cisungu, this guide should provide you a concise outline for getting your new language learners to master the basic structure of the Cisungu language.

Modern Cisungu is a spelling system for Cisungu that uses spaces to make Cisungu easier to read. It is the spelling system used in this book.

Before you jump in ...

In the text, any text marked with * indicates ungrammatical usage. Bolded text can be looked up in the index. The guide attempts to use plain English the first time a concept is explained; in this case the technical term is included in square brackets.

Pronunciations are surrounded by /... / signs.

Written form	a
Spoken form	/a/

English translations are placed in italics in [ ] near their Cisungu renditions.

Let's go!

We hope that this guide will help open up the culture of the Cisungu-speaking peoples all over the world to you!

Go on and be free in Cisungu!

All the words you need

These are the only words you need to know to understand Modern Cisungu as described in this book.

Of course, there are many more words in Cisungu. Get the Modern Cisungu Dictionary to learn more Cisungu words!

~ ~ ~

musuma *(adj)* good

muntu *(nom.1)* person

ine *(pro)* I

temwa *(act)* love

lya *(act)* eat

(det) the

ichakulya *(nom)* food

mailo *(adv)* tomorrow

isa *(act)* come

ng'anda *(nom)* home

mulumendo *(nom.1)* boy

mukashana *(nom)* girl

fwaya *(act)* want

Read Modern Cisungu

~ ~ ~

mukashana *(nom)* girl

mbwa *(nom)* dog

muti *(nom)* tree

ing'anda *(nom)* house

 (det) a

 (det) the

musuma *(adj.1)* good

buta *(adj)* white

umo *(adj)* one

kote *(adj)* old

cipya *(adj)* new

fita *(adj)* black

wandi *(pos.1)* my

obe *(pos)* your

wakwe *(pos.1)* her

we *(pos.1)* our

enu *(pos)* your

abo *(pos)* their

wakwe *(pos.1)* his

ine *(pro)* I

iwe *(pro)* you

uyu *(pro)* she

uyu *(pro)* he

ifwe *(pro)* we

imwe *(pro)* you

aba *(pro)* they

langa *(act)* show

icifulo *(nom)* position

nshita *(nom)* time

incende *(nom)* place

pa *(pre)* on

pa *(pre)* at

mukati *(pre)* inside

kunuma *(pre)* behind

micitile *(nom)* action

temwa *(act)* love

ipusha *(act)* ask

lya *(act)* eat

nwa *(act)* drink

isa *(act)* come

wikala *(act)* sit

lelo *(adv)* today

mailo *(adv)* tomorrow

incende *(nom)* place

eko *(adv)* there

mulumendo *(nom.1)* boy

bulondoloshi *(nom)* statement

peela *(act)* give

ukwi shibisha *(nom)* information

ichakulya *(nom)* food

cebo *(nom.1)* command

(det) a

amba *(act)* start

bwipusho *(nom)* question

senda *(act)* get

ee *(exc)* yes

awe *(exc)* no

nshi *(pro)* what

Write Modern Cisungu

Writing and speaking are different. We write with Modern Cisungu spelling. We speak with different voices and accents. Accents are usually tied to places and so you can tell where someone grew up just by their accent!

Spelling

The following spelling conventions are supported by the Cisungu spellchecker available from kasahorow.

Write for comprehension

1. Do not use accents on top of vowels [diacritics]. Instead structure your sentences to avoid ambiguity.

2. Do not use slang or shortened phrases forms. Instead use full forms to make your text easier to read by new readers.

Importing foreign words

This is a 2-stage process. When words are deemed to have made the transition from specialised terminology into popu- lar us- age, this process should be applied to revise the spelling of the word accordingly.

1. **Specialised terminology**: Import into Cisungu specialised terminology unlikely to come into popular usage with- out a change of spelling. This eliminates the possibil- ity of ambiguity for specialists who are already familiar with the term. It is good practice to indicate the origin language of the specialized terminology.

2. **Popular usage terminology**: Phonetically render into Cisungu new words that are in popular usage or likely to come into popular usage. Use the phonetic preference of the largest city where you can find the most Cisungu speakers. When doing so, stick to the pronunciation pat- tern of the original language. This enables readers who encounter the word for the first time in writing to pro- nounce the word in a way that will confirm to their ears that it is indeed not an uncommon term.

Punctuation

Words are separated by spaces and other symbols.
These are the most common symbols and their meanings:

.	Shows the end of a statement. Also used to separate the whole number and the fraction components of a decimal number like 1.23
?	Shows the end of a question

!	Shows the end of a command
,	Shows a short pause
:	Shows a longer pause than a comma

~ ~ ~

lemba *(act)* write

landa *(act)* speak

ba *(act)* be

pusanya *(adj)* different

ifwe *(pro)* we

Speaking Cisungu

This is a guide for how to read and write Cisungu. We include this section to remind you that the best way to learn how to speak Cisungu is by chatting with someone who grew up speaking Cisungu. kasahorow has communities online where you can meet and befriend people who already speak Cisungu.

Search for **Cisungu kasahorow** on the Internet and join a language group.

Remember that written Modern Cisungu is for keeping records in easy to read Cisungu. It is just the beginning of your Cisungu knowledge.

1. So go make a friend who speaks Cisungu.

2. Speak to them only in Cisungu

3. And they speak to you in Cisungu

For reference, here are the sounds of spoken Cisungu

- vowels: a e i o u

- consonants: b ch d f g j k l m n ŋ ɲ p s sh t w y

23

When you have learned the pronunciation of the basic vocabulary in a *Modern Cisungu Dictionary*, you should be able to follow spoken Cisungu. If after memorizing the pronunciation of basic vocabulary you still cannot follow spoken Cisungu, ask your friend to slow down their rate of talking.

At the slower speed, you should be able to pick up enough words to make sense of what they are saying.

The world is waiting for you to speak your first Cisungu sentence with confidence!

~ ~ ~

cibusa *(nom)* friend

ululimi *(nom)* language

pamo *(nom)* group

lundinkanya *(act)* join

Use These Words

You now know the most common sentence patterns in Cisungu.

This section provides basic vocabulary to help you expand the range of things you can say.

Simple Pronouns

- ine [*I*]
- iwe [*you*]
- uyu [*she*]
- uyu [*he*]
- ifwe [*we*]
- imwe [*you*]
- aba [*they*]

Ownership

- wandi [*my*]
- obe [*your*]

- wakwe [*her*]

- wakwe [*his*]

- we [*our*]

- enu [*your*]

- abo [*their*]

Nouns

- mukashana [*girl*]

- mulumendo [*boy*]

- muntu [*person*]

- mbwa [*dog*]

- inama [*animal*]

- atomu [*atom*]

- muti [*tree*]

- ing'anda [*house*]

- sukulu [*school*]

- ichakulya [*food*]

Adjectives

- musuma [*good*]
- buta [*white*]
- umo [*one*]
- kote [*old*]
- cipya [*new*]

Verbs

- temwa (ukutemwa) [*love (to love)*]
- fwaya (ukufwaya) [*want (to want)*]
- lya (ukulya) [*eat (to eat)*]
- nwa (ukunwa) [*drink (to drink)*]
- isa (ukuisa) [*come (to come)*]
- wikala (ukuwikala) [*sit (to sit)*]

Adverbs

- lelo [*today*]
- mailo [*tomorrow*]
- mailo [*yesterday*]
- pano [*here*]
- eko [*there*]

Conjunctions

- 1 na 2 [*1 and 2*]
- 1 atemwa 2 [*1 or 2*]

Exclamations

- ee [*yes*]
- awe [*no*]

Basic Ideas

Numbers

The international number system is based on multiples of the number ten [*decimal*].

- 0 - zero
- 1 - umo
- 2 - bili
- 3 - tatu
- 4 - ne
- 5 - sano
- 6 - mutanda
- 7 - cine lubali
- 8 - cine konse konse

- 9 - pabula
- 10 - ikumi
- 11 - ikumi na umo
- 12 - ikumi na bili
- 13 - ikumi na tatu
- 14 - ikumi na ne
- 15 - ikumi na sano
- 16 - ikumi na mutanda
- 17 - ikumi na cine lubali
- 18 - ikumi na cine konse konse
- 19 - ikumi na pabula
- 20 - amakumi yabili
- 21 - amakumi yabili-na-umo
- 22 - amakumi yabili-na-bili
- 30 - makumi yatatu
- 40 - makumi yane
- 50 - makumi yasano
- 60 - makumi mutanda
- 70 - makumi cine lubali
- 80 - makumi cine konse konse
- 90 - makumi pabula

- 100 - umo mwanda
- 1000 - umo alufu
- 1/2 - pakati
- 1/3 - umo bwa tatu
- 2/3 - bili bwa tatu
- 3/20 - tatu bwa amakumi yabili

Time

A day has 24 hours. A year has 365 days or 366 days.

- fitulukila [*dawn*]
- akacelo [*morning*]
- cungulo [*afternoon*]
- cungulopo [*evening*]
- bushiku [*night*]

Days of the week

According to the international standard ISO 8601, Monday is the first day of the modern week.

- Pali Cimo [*Monday*]
- Pali Cibili [*Tuesday*]
- Pali Citatu [*Wednesday*]
- Pali Cine [*Thursday*]

- Pali Cisano [*Friday*]
- Pa Cibelushi [*Saturday*]
- Pa Mulungu [*Sunday*]

Months of the year

The international year is divided into 12 months.

- Kabengele kanono [*January*]
- Kabengele kakalamba [*February*]
- Kutumpu [*March*]
- Shinde [*April*]
- Kapepo kanono [*May*]
- Kapepo kakalamba [*June*]
- Cikungulupepo [*July*]
- Kasakantobo [*August*]
- Lusuba lunono [*September*]
- Langashe [*October*]
- Cinshikubili [*November*]
- Mupundu-milimo [*December*]

So, here are some dates.

- Pali Citatu. Kutumpu 6, 1957 [*Wednesday. March 6, 1957*]
- Pali Cisano. Cikungulupepo 1, 1960 [*Friday. July 1, 1960*]

- Pali Cimo. Cinshikubili 20, 2000 [*Monday. November 20, 2000*]

- Pali Cibili. Kabengele kanono 1, 2030 [*Tuesday. January 1, 2030*]

Directions

- icisansa ku kuso [*left hand*]

- icisansa lungamika [*right hand*]

- ukuisa pano [*to come here*]

- ukuya eko [*to go there*]

- kapinda ka kukuso [*north*]

- kapinda ka kulyo [*south*]

- kukabanga [*east*]

- masamba [*west*]

Food

- ichakulya [*food*]

- amenshi [*water*]

- inama [*meat*]

- isabi [*fish*]

- cani [*plant*]

Transport

- icinga [*bicycle*]
- motoka [*car*]
- shitima [*train*]
- indeke [*aeroplane*]

Colours

- fita [*black*]
- kashika [*red*]
- umutuntula [*yellow*]
- katapa katapa [*green*]
- makumbi makumbi [*blue*]
- buta [*white*]

Family

- ulupwa [*family*]
- mayo [*mum*]
- tata [*father*]
- umwaice [*kid*]
- mulumendo [*boy*]
- mukashana [*girl*]
- bayamaba [*uncle*]
- ba [*aunt*]

Occupations

- mulimi [*farmer*]

- umulondo [*fisherman*]

- muleshi [*nurse*]

- dokotala [*doctor*]

- kafundisha [*teacher*]

- kalemba [*writer*]

- shimakwebo [*trader*]

- shimapepo [*priest*]

- mfumu [*chief*]

Actions

You will frequently use the simple present tense of the verb "to be". We conjugate it here for your convenience.

- ine ndaba [*I am*]

- iwe ulaba [*you are*]

- uyu alaba [*she is*]

- uyu alaba [*he is*]

- ta alaba [*it is*]

- ifwe tulaba [*we are*]

- imwe mulaba [*you are*]

- aba balaba [*they are*]

Here are frequently opposing verbs in the form that you'll find in kasahorow dictionaries.

- isa [*come*]
- ya [*go*]
- lya [*eat*]
- nwa [*drink*]
- belenga [*read*]
- lemba [*write*]
- peela [*give*]
- twala [*take*]
- sunka [*push*]
- tinta [*pull*]

Verbs can be modified by adverbs such as *bwangu.* Here are some examples:

- isa bwangu [*come quickly*]
- ya bwangu [*go quickly*]
- lya bwangu [*eat quickly*]
- nwa bwangu [*drink quickly*]
- belenga bwangu [*read quickly*]
- lemba bwangu [*write quickly*]
- peela bwangu [*give quickly*]
- twala bwangu [*take quickly*]

Write and speak Cisungu!

With your new knowledge and a modern Cisungu dictionary, you should be able to translate modern Cisungu words and read them aloud with the accent your Cisungu friend taught you.

~ ~ ~

ine *(pro)* I

iwe *(pro)* you

uyu *(pro)* she

uyu *(pro)* he

ifwe *(pro)* we

imwe *(pro)* you

aba *(pro)* they

wandi *(pos.1)* my

obe *(pos)* your

wakwe *(pos.1)* her

wakwe *(pos.1)* his

we *(pos.1)* our

enu *(pos)* your

abo *(pos)* their

mukashana *(nom)* girl

mulumendo *(nom.1)* boy

muntu *(nom.1)* person

mbwa *(nom)* dog

inama *(nom)* animal

muti *(nom)* tree

ing'anda *(nom)* house

sukulu *(nom.0)* school

ichakulya *(nom)* food

musuma *(adj.1)* good

buta *(adj)* white

umo *(adj)* one

kote *(adj)* old

cipya *(adj)* new

temwa *(act)* love

fwaya *(act)* want

lya *(act)* eat

nwa *(act)* drink

isa *(act)* come

wikala *(act)* sit

lelo *(adv)* today

mailo *(adv)* tomorrow

eko *(adv)* there

ee *(exc)* yes

awe *(exc)* no

zero *(adj)* zero

bili *(adj)* two

tatu *(adj)* three

ne *(adj)* four

sano *(adj)* five

mutanda *(adj)* six

cine lubali *(adj)* seven

cine konse konse *(adj)* eight

pabula *(adj)* nine

ikumi *(adj)* ten

ikumi na umo *(adj)* eleven

ikumi na bili *(adj)* twelve

ikumi na tatu *(adj)* thirteen

ikumi na ne *(adj)* fourteen

ikumi na sano *(adj)* fifteen

ikumi na mutanda *(adj)* sixteen

ikumi na cine lubali *(adj)* seventeen

ikumi na cine konse konse *(adj)* eighteen

ikumi na pabula *(adj)* nineteen

amakumi yabili *(num)* twenty

umo *(num)* one

bili *(num)* two

makumi yatatu *(adj)* thirty

makumi yane *(adj)* forty

makumi yasano *(adj)* fifty

makumi mutanda *(adj)* sixty

makumi cine lubali *(adj)* seventy

makumi cine konse konse *(adj)* eighty

makumi pabula *(adj)* ninety

mwanda *(num)* hundred

alufu *(num)* thousand

pakati *(nom)* half

amakumi yabili *(adj)* twenty

nshita *(nom)* time

(det) a

ubushiku *(nom)* day

kwata *(act)* have

24 *(num)* 24

nsa *(nom)* hour

mwaka *(nom)* year

365 *(num)* 365

366 *(num)* 366

fitulukila *(nom)* dawn

akacelo *(nom)* morning

cungulo *(nom)* afternoon

cungulopo *(nom)* evening

bushiku *(nom)* night

Pali Cimo *(nom)* Monday

Pali Cibili *(nom)* Tuesday

Pali Citatu *(nom)* Wednesday

Pali Cine *(nom)* Thursday

Pali Cisano *(nom)* Friday

Pa Cibelushi *(nom)* Saturday

Pa Mulungu *(nom)* Sunday

Kabengele kanono *(nom)* January

Kabengele kakalamba *(nom)* February

Kapepo kanono *(nom)* May

Kapepo kakalamba *(nom)* June

Cikungulupepo *(nom)* July

Kasakantobo *(nom)* August

Lusuba lunono *(nom)* September

Langashe *(nom)* October

Cinshikubili *(nom)* November

Mupundu-milimo *(nom)* December

ku kuso *(adj)* left

icisansa *(nom)* hand

lungamika *(adj)* right

ya *(act)* go

kapinda ka kukuso *(nom)* north

kapinda ka kulyo *(nom.1)* south

kukabanga *(nom)* east

masamba *(nom)* west

amenshi *(nom)* water

inama *(nom)* meat

isabi *(nom)* fish

cani *(nom)* plant

icinga *(nom)* bicycle

motoka *(nom.2)* car

shitima *(nom.4)* train

indeke *(nom.1)* aeroplane

fita *(adj)* black

kashika *(adj)* red

umutuntula *(adj)* yellow

katapa katapa *(adj)* green

makumbi makumbi *(adj)* blue

ulupwa *(nom)* family

mayo *(nom)* mum

tata *(nom.1)* father

umwaice *(nom.1)* kid

bayamaba *(nom)* uncle

ba *(nom)* aunt

mulimi *(nom.1)* farmer

umulondo *(nom)* fisherman

muleshi *(nom)* nurse

dokotala *(nom)* doctor

kafundisha *(nom)* teacher

kalemba *(nom)* writer

shimakwebo *(nom)* trader

shimapepo *(nom)* priest

mfumu *(nom.1)* chief

ba *(act)* be

ta *(pro)* it

belenga *(act)* read

lemba *(act)* write

peela *(act)* give

twala *(act)* take

sunka *(act)* push

tinta *(act)* pull

Basic Cisungu Reading

Read and translate this Cisungu poem.

Umutwe, Icipeya, Ikufi Na Utukondo

Umutwe, icipeya, ikufi na utukondo.
Umutwe, icipeya, ikufi na utukondo.

Linso, kutwi, umoona na akanwa.

Umutwe, icipeya, ikufi na utukondo.
Ikufi na utukondo.

    Well done! Thank you!

~ ~ ~

belenga *(act)* read

uyu *(det)* this

umutwe *(nom)* head

icipeya *(nom.1)* shoulder

ikufi *(nom)* knee

utukondo *(nom.3)* toe

kutwi *(nom)* ear

umoona *(nom)* nose

akanwa *(nom)* mouth

mwabombenipo *(exc)* well done

natotela *(exc)* thank you

Basic Cisungu Phrases

Remember these handy phrases to get you out of a tight spot.

Greetings

- shani [hello]

- mwaiseni [welcome]

- Ine ndaba kafundisha. [I am a teacher.]

- shalapo [goodbye]

Respect

- natotela [thank you]

- mukwai [please]

- nakaana [sorry]

Request

- Ishina obe alaba nshi? [What is your name?]
- Pakuti alaba nshi? [What is that?]

Answer

- ee [yes]
- awe [no]

~ ~ ~

shani *(exc)* hello

mwaiseni *(exc)* welcome

ine *(pro)* I

ba *(act)* be

(det) a

kafundisha *(nom)* teacher

shalapo *(exc)* goodbye

natotela *(exc)* thank you

mukwai *(adv)* please

nakaana *(exc)* sorry

obe *(pos)* your

ishina *(nom.1.4)* name

nshi *(pro)* what

pakuti *(det)* that

ee *(exc)* yes

awe *(exc)* no

Basic Cisungu Translation

Ilul Chibemba na iwe ukasambilila Chibemba.

1. _____
   ing'anda buta

2. _____
   ine ndatemwa Efia

3. _____
   iwe ulatemwa Efia

4. _____
   uyu alatemwa Efia

5. _____
   ifwe tulatemwa Efia

6. _____
   imwe mulatemwa Efia

7. _____
   aba balatemwa Efia

8. _____
   ine nlyile ichakulya

9. _____
   iwe ulyile ichakulya

10. _____
    uyu alyile ichakulya

11. _____
    uyu alyile ichakulya

12. _____
    ine alyile ichakulya

13. _____
    ifwe tulyile ichakulya

14. _____
    imwe mulyile ichakulya

15. _____
    aba balyile ichakulya

16. _____
    ine nkaisa ng'anda, mailo

17. _____
    iwe ukaisa ng'anda, mailo

18. _____
    uyu akaisa ng'anda, mailo

19. _____
    uyu akaisa ng'anda, mailo

20. _____
    ta akaisa ng'anda, mailo

21. _____
    ifwe tukaisa ng'anda, mailo

22. _____
    imwe mukaisa ng'anda, mailo

23. _____
    aba bakaisa ng'anda, mailo

24. _____
    iwe na ine

25. _____
    iwe na ine tukabelenga

26. _____
    iwe na ine tukabelenga bwangu

27. _____
    iwe na ine tukabelenga icitabo

28. _____
    iwe na ine tukabelenga bwangu icitabo

29. _____
    ine ndaba muntu musuma

30. _____
    iwe ulaba muntu musuma

31. _____
    Efia alaba muntu musuma

~ ~ ~

iwe *(pro)* you

sambilila *(act)* learn

buta *(adj)* white

ing'anda *(nom)* house

ine *(pro)* I

temwa *(act)* love

uyu *(pro)* he

ifwe *(pro)* we

imwe *(pro)* you

aba *(pro)* they

lya *(act)* eat

(det) the

ichakulya *(nom)* food

uyu *(pro)* she

isa *(act)* come

ng'anda *(nom)* home

mailo *(adv)* tomorrow

ta *(pro)* it

belenga *(act)* read

(det) a

icitabo *(nom)* book

ba *(act)* be

musuma *(adj.1)* good

muntu *(nom.1)* person

Chibemba-English

a b c d e f g h i j k l m n ɲ ŋ o p r s t u v w y z

Ø *(det)* the

Ø *(det)* a

bwa a ya lwa *(pre.1)* of

aba *(pro)* they

Aba *(din.1)* Aba

aba *(pro)* these

abafyashi *(nom.1)* parents

abantu abantu *(nom)* people

abashilika *(nom)* warriors

suma *(adj)* pretty

Abena *(nom.1)* Abena

abena Roma *(nom)* Romans

abo *(pos)* their

adelesi *(nom)* address

ademe *(nom)* ademe

afghan *(nom.1)* Afghan

Afghanistan *(nom.1)* Afghanistan

afwa *(nom)* help

afwa *(act)* assist

afwa *(act)* help

afwa *(nom.1)* favour

agbayun *(nom.1)* Synsepalum dulcificum

air conditioner *(nom.1)* air-conditioner

Ajoa *(nom.1)* Ajoa

aka kuntanshi kumabele *(nom)* nipple

akabulungwa *(nom.1)* organism

akabungwe *(nom)* committee

akabungwe *(nom)* association

akabungwe *(nom)* organization

akabungwe kamapolitikisi *(nom)* political party

akacelo *(nom)* morning

akakopo *(nom)* tin

umunwe akakumo *(nom)* finger

akalefu *(nom)* cheek

akalumba *(nom)* lightning

icimuti akamuti *(nom)* stick

akani Akan *(kw)* Akan

akana *(nom.1)* share

akana kang'ombe *(nom)* calf

akanono *(adj)* smaller

akanono *(adj)* minor

akanono *(adj)* tiny

akanwa akanwa *(nom)* mouth

akanya *(act)* share

kanya akanya *(nom)* baby

akapinda kakukulyo *(adj)* northern

akapuna *(nom)* stool

akaputula kamukati *(nom)* underwear

akasakantobo *(nom)* spring

akasakantobo *(nom)* Autumn

akasalu *(nom)* handkerchief

akashishi *(nom)* insect

akashishi *(nom)* virus

iakasuba akasuba *(nom)* sun

akaswende *(nom.1)* herpes

akatende *(nom.1)* heel

wakwe akwe *(pos.1)* her

wakwe akwe *(pos.1)* his

algebra *(nom.1)* algebra

Algeria *(nom.1)* Algeria

algorithm *(nom.1)* algorithm

alufu *(adj)* thousand

Ama *(nom.1)* Ama

amabula *(nom)* foliage

amafi *(nom)* feces

amafi *(nom)* poop

amafi *(nom)* faeces

amafisa kanwa *(nom.1)* corruption

mafunde amafunde *(nom)* policy

amafuta yamishishi *(nom)* pomade

amafya *(nom)* consequence

amaka amaka *(nom)* strength

amaka *(nom)* authority

amaka *(nom)* power

amaka *(nom.1)* vim

amaka *(adj)* powerful

amakumi yabili *(adj)* twenty

amakwebo makwebo *(nom)* business

amalasha *(nom.1)* charcoal

amale *(nom)* millet

Amalinya *(kw)* Amharic

amalipilo *(nom.1)* fees

amalipilo *(nom)* compensation

amano *(act)* sense

amano *(nom)* sense

amano *(nom)* prudence

amano *(nom)* knowledge

amapange *(nom.1)* objective

amapange *(nom)* plans

amapange ipange *(nom)* plan

amapendo *(nom.1)* accounting

amapinda *(nom)* Proverbs

amasako *(nom)* feather

amasambililo amasambililo *(nom)* education

amatako *(nom)* buttocks

amatamba *(nom)* storm

itamba amatamba *(nom)* wave

amatunko *(nom)* temptation

amba *(act)* begin

amba *(act)* start

ambasada *(nom.1)* ambassador

ameni *(exc)* amen

amenshi *(nom)* water

amenshi yakosa *(nom)* ice

america *(nom.1)* America

American *(adj)* American

amfula *(act)* crow

wandi andi lyandi *(pos.1)* my

andi *(pro)* mine

angala *(adj)* entertaining

angala *(nom)* play

angala *(act)* play

angufyanya *(act)* fast

anguka *(adj)* simple

anguka *(adj)* easy

anguka *(adj)* lightweight

aniseed *(nom.1)* aniseed

antartica *(nom.1)* Antartica

aplikoti *(nom)* apricot

apple *(nom)* apple

Arabiya *(nom.1)* Arabic

ashima *(act)* borrow

ashima *(act)* lend

atemwa *(cjn)* or

Atlantiki *(adj)* Atlantic

atomu *(sci)* atom

aula *(act)* yawn

awe *(exc)* no

awe *(adj)* no

ayo *(exc)* ayo

ba *(act)* be

ba *(nom)* mister

ba *(nom.1)* miss

ba *(nom)* aunt

ba bwino *(act)* be good

ba namaka *(adj)* able

ba nomulandu *(nom)* guilt

ba politishani fanganinina *(nom)* politician

ba umutali *(act)* be lengthy

ba uwakulekelesha *(act)* be last

babili *(adj)* both

babu *(act)* barb

backlog *(nom.1)* backlog

bafundi *(nom)* art

cinungi bala *(nom)* porcupine

baluni *(nom.0)* balloon

bambi *(det)* some

bampundu *(nom.1)* twins

bani *(pro)* whose

banjo *(nom)* guitar

banka *(nom.1)* banker

banki *(nom.0)* bank

banomweo *(act)* live

basa *(nom)* plane

basi *(nom.0)* bus

inkombe bataki *(nom)* messenger

tatu *(adj)* three

baule *(nom)* Baule

bayamaba *(nom)* uncle

beka *(pro)* themselves

belama *(act)* hide

belebensa *(adj)* strange

belela *(act)* adopt

belelela *(adj)* everlasting

belenga *(act)* read

bemba *(nom)* sea

Bemba *(nom)* lake

bemba mukalamba bemba *(nom)* ocean

bena *(pro)* them

bendela *(nom)* flag

ubucende benkani *(nom)* adultery

bepa *(act)* cheat

bepa *(act)* lie

bepesha *(act)* accuse

bɛnkan sɛbɛn *(nom.1)* contract

bi *(adj)* bad

bika *(nom)* set

bika *(act)* put

bika *(nom)* beaker

bika *(nom.1)* deposit

bila *(act)* sew

bile mbila *(nom)* proclamation

bili *(adj)* two

bilioni *(adj)* billion

bipa *(nom)* greed

bipa *(adj)* ugly

bishi *(adj)* raw

blog *(nom)* blog

bola *(act)* rot

bomba *(nom)* bomb

bomba *(nom)* working

bomba *(adj)* wet

bomba *(act)* work

bomba *(adj)* soaked

ukubomba bomba *(nom)* work

bomba capamo *(nom)* coop-
eration

bombesha *(nom.1)* hardwork

bomfya *(act)* use

bomfya *(act)* wield

bonse *(det)* all

bonse *(pro)* everyone

bonsefye *(pro)* each and everyone

bosa *(act)* bark

braketi *(nom)* bracket

Brazzaville *(nom.1)* Congo-Brazzaville

brown *(adj)* brown

bubenshi *(nom.5)* ant

bubi *(nom)* evil

bubi bubi *(adv)* wrongly

buce buce *(adv)* slowly

bucenjeshi *(adj)* cunning

ubuci buci *(nom)* honey

bucibinda *(nom)* skill

bucilolo *(nom.1)* bishop

bucindami *(nom)* dignitary

bucingo *(nom)* obstacle

bucishinka *(nom)* honesty

bucushi *(nom)* passion

budget *(nom.1)* budget

bufumo *(nom)* width

bufundi ɲɛɛ *(nom)* efficiency

buka *(act)* wake

bukankala *(nom)* prosperity

bukata lawasali *(nom)* glory

bukota *(nom.1)* advocate

bukulu *(nom)* breadth

bukwebo *(nom.1)* commerce

bula *(nom.2)* page

bulalo *(nom)* bridge

bulanda *(adj)* sad

bulanda *(nom)* sorrow

bulanda bulanda *(adj)* miserly

bulendo *(nom)* trip

bulili *(adj)* greedy

bulondoloshi *(nom)* statement

buloshi *(nom.1)* witchcraft

bululu *(nom)* relative

bulungu *(nom)* bead

bulwele *(nom)* sickness

bum *(nom)* bum

bumi *(nom)* life

bundama *(adj)* cloudy

bunga *(nom)* flour

bunonshi ubunonshi *(nom)* wealth

bunte *(nom)* testimony

buntungwa *(nom.1)* independence

bununko *(nom.1)* smell

bupe *(nom.1)* award

bupe *(nom)* gift

bupute *(nom)* accountability

busangu *(nom)* treason

busanso *(nom)* danger

bushiku *(nom)* night

bushiku bwaku tusha *(nom)*

holiday

busomboshi *(nom)* harvest

busuma *(nom)* beauty

busuma *(adj)* bountiful

buta *(adj)* white

buta *(nom.1)* bow

buta *(adj)* bright

butali janya *(nom)* height

butali *(nom)* length

buteko *(nom.1)* administration

butuka *(act)* run

butuluka *(adj)* grey

buyantanshi *(nom)* progress

buyantanshi *(nom.1)* development

buyo *(nom)* objective

bwafya *(nom.1)* trouble

bwalwa *(nom)* beer

bwangalo *(nom)* drama

bwangalo *(nom)* sport

bwangalo *(nom)* game

bwangu *(adv)* quickly

bwasuko *(nom)* response

bwasuko *(nom)* answer

bwekeshapo *(act)* repeat

bwela *(act)* return

bwelelo *(nom)* forgiveness

bwesha *(act)* reply

bwesha *(act)* decrease

bwile *(nom.1)* riddle

bwina buntu *(nom)* race

bwingi *(adj)* more

bwingi *(adj)* plentiful

bwino *(adj)* reliable

bwino *(adj)* well

bwino *(adj)* normal

bwino *(adj)* better

bwino bwino *(adv)* clearly

bwipusho *(nom)* question

byala *(act)* sow

byala *(act)* plant

byola *(act)* belch

ca bubili *(nom)* second

cabu *(nom)* port

cakufwala *(nom)* garment

cakufwala *(nom.1)* dress

cakunwa minfɛn *(nom)* drink

calembwa *(nom)* article

calici *(nom)* church

California *(nom)* California

calo *(nom)* world

Cameroon *(nom.1)* Cameroon

Canada *(nom)* Canada

cani *(nom)* plant

capa *(act)* wash

capwa *(adj)* empty

catarrh *(nom)* catarrh

cawama *(adj)* nice

cebo *(nom.1)* command

cedi *(nom.1)* cedi

cefya *(act)* reduce

cefya *(act)* shrink

ceki *(nom.1)* cheque

cela *(sci)* iron

celeta *(nom.1)* chariot

celwa *(act)* delay

cena *(act)* injure

cena *(nom.1)* foul

ceni *(nom.1)* chain

cenjela *(adj)* smart

ccpa *(adj)* little

cetekela *(act)* trust

cetekela *(act)* believe

cetekela tetekela *(nom)* trust

cɛmisɛn *(nom.1)* young boy

umushipi cɛsiri jala *(nom)* belt

chali *(adv)* as

chiBemba *(kw)* Bemba

chimpanzi *(nom.1)* chimpanzee

china *(nom.1)* China

chipumbu *(adj)* foolish

choko *(nom.1)* chalk

chokwe *(nom)* Chokwe

chopa *(nom)* helicopter

cibinda *(adj)* responsible

cibubi *(nom)* cataract

cibubi *(nom)* eyeball

cibukisho *(nom)* memory

cibulu *(adj)* mute

cibulu *(nom.1)* mute

cibusa *(nom)* friend

ng'anda cifulo *(nom)* home

cifwaika *(nom)* priority

cikabilila *(act)* heat

cikankala *(adj)* important

cikuko *(nom)* plague

cikuku *(adj)* gentle

cikulu *(adj)* major

cikumo *(nom.1)* thumb

Cikungulupepo *(nom)* July

cila *(adv)* more

cilayo *(nom)* promise

cilemba *(nom)* bean

cilenga *(nom)* effect

cilila *(act)* pass by

cilola *(nom)* mirror

cilolo *(nom)* prince

cilumba *(adj)* arrogant

cilumba *(nom)* arrogance

cilya *(pro)* that

cilya ca cangufyanya bwangu *(exc)* that escalated quickly

cimbi *(adj)* other

cimbi *(adj)* another

cimbusu *(nom)* toilet

cimbwi *(nom)* hyena

cimfya *(nom)* victory

cimo *(pro)* one

cimocine *(adj)* same

cimuntu *(nom)* giant

cimuntu *(adj)* giant

cindamikwa *(nom)* royalty

cindika *(act)* respect

cindikwa *(nom.1)* excellence

cine *(adj)* real

cine cine *(adv)* frankly

cine konse konse *(adj)* eight

cine lubali *(adj)* seven

cinja *(nom)* affect

cinja *(act)* bleach

cinja ilangi *(nom)* dye

cinseketa *(nom.1)* cheetah

Cinshikubili *(nom)* November

icinso cinso *(nom.1.4)* face

cintu *(nom.1)* something

icintu cintu *(nom)* thing

cintu *(pro)* something

cinyantilo *(adj)* sole

cinyantilo *(nom)* sole

cipatala *(nom)* hospital

cipembele *(nom)* rhino

cipesha mano *(nom)* mystery

cipingo *(nom)* bible

cipululu *(nom.1)* owl

cipuna sofa *(nom)* sofa

cipunda *(nom)* hole

cipute *(act)* boil

ciputulwa camubili *(nom.1)* organ

cipya *(adj)* new

cisali *(nom.1)* cane

cisankano *(nom)* market

cisendo *(nom.1)* burden

cishibisho *(nom)* advertisement

cishishi *(nom)* beetle

cisote *(nom)* hat

cisote ca mfumu *(nom.1)* crown

cisubilo *(nom)* aspiration

cisuma *(adv)* well

cisuma *(nom)* right

Cisungu Icisungu *(kw)* English

ciswebebe *(nom)* desert

cita *(act)* pursue

cita *(nom)* act

cita *(nom)* sacrifice

cita *(act)* do

cita *(aux)* can

citambala *(nom.4)* towel

citendekelo *(nom)* beginning

citeshoni citeshoni *(nom)* station

citika *(act)* happen

citika kuntanshi *(nom)* destiny

citumbi *(nom.1)* corpse

citwalo *(nom)* fruit

ciwelewele *(nom)* imbecile

kwishilya ciya *(nom)* harbour

clalion *(adj)* clarion

clove *(nom)* clove

musango cogoya *(nom)* technique

cokoleti *(nom)* chocolate

colwa *(nom.2)* zebra

cona *(nom)* cat

conse *(adj)* whole

conse pamo *(nom)* amount

cula *(act)* suffer

cula *(nom)* frog

cuma *(nom)* treasure

cungulo *(nom)* noon

cungulo *(nom)* afternoon

cungulopo *(nom)* evening

cungulopo mukwai *(exc)* good afternoon

cusha *(act)* persecute

cymbol *(nom)* cymbal

tasha dansɛ *(nom)* congratulations

demokalashi *(nom)* democracy

dikishonari *(nom.0)* dictionary

dinozɔri *(nom.1)* dinosaur

dokotala *(nom)* doctor

dollar *(nom.1)* dollar

nono dɔɔni *(nom)* little

dukɔfɛla *(nom.1)* backyard

dula *(adj)* expensive

dvd *(nom)* DVD

dyonko *(nom)* bonus

ee *(exc)* yes

eka *(adj)* only

eko *(adv)* there

elyo *(cjn)* then

email email *(nom)* email

ena *(pro)* him

ena eka *(pro)* himself

kuka *(act)* travel

enda *(act)* walk

endesha *(act)* hurry

England *(nom)* England

ensha *(act)* drive

imwe enu *(pro)* yours

enu *(pos)* your

esha *(nom)* test

we esu *(pos.1)* our

evangelyo *(nom)* gospel

ewe *(nom)* ewe

fika *(act)* reach

fika *(act)* arrive

fika *(act)* approach

filimu *(nom)* movie

filyafine *(adj)* actual

fimba *(nom)* slate

fimba *(act)* cover

fimo *(pro)* some

fina *(nom.1)* weight

fina *(adj)* heavy

fisama *(nom)* hide

fisha amashiwi *(act)* report

fita *(adj)* black

fita *(adj)* dark

fitulukila *(nom)* dawn

foloko *(nom.0)* fork

foni *(nom.0)* telephone

icibansa foro *(nom)* playing field

fube fube *(nom)* mist

fubefube *(nom.1)* fog

fukauka *(nom)* oasis

fula *(nom)* Fula

fulinti *(nom)* flint

fulwa *(nom)* frustration

fulwe *(nom)* tortoise

fuma *(adv)* out

fuma *(act)* leave

fuma *(act)* log out

icifumamo fumamo *(nom)* result

fumineko *(adj)* previous

fumo *(adj)* pregnant

fumya *(act)* withdraw

fumya *(act)* remove

funda *(act)* teach

funde *(nom)* law

fungaula *(nom)* squash

fusha *(nom)* multiplication

fwa *(adj)* dead

fwa *(act)* die

fwaikwa *(nom.1)* demand

fwaka *(nom.1)* cigarette

fwaka fwaka *(nom)* tobacco

fwala *(act)* wear

fwaya *(act)* want

fwaya *(act)* wish

fwaya *(adj)* desirable

fwaya *(act)* seek

fwaya *(act)* search

fwaya mako *(nom)* need

kukabila fwaya *(nom)* wish

fwile *(act)* deserve

fwile *(nom)* worth

fwile *(act)* need

fwilefye *(adv)* obviously

fyabo *(pro)* theirs

fyachabe chabe *(adj)* unnecessary

fyala *(nom)* inlaw

fyalwa *(nom.1)* birth

fyalwa *(act)* birth

fyanunkila *(nom)* perfume

fye *(adv)* just

fye *(adj)* mere

fyompa *(nom)* kiss

fyonse *(pro)* everything

fyonse *(adj)* all

Gadangme *(nom.1)* GaDangme

gallon *(nom)* gallon

gandhi *(din)* Gandhi

garden-egg *(nom)* garden egg

gari *(nom)* gari

garlic *(nom)* garlic

gasi *(nom.1)* gas

Ghana *(nom.1)* Ghana

gilepu *(nom.1)* grape

Guinea Bissau *(nom)* Guinea-Bissau

haleluya *(exc)* hallelujah

harmattan *(nom)* harmattan

hashtag *(nom.1)* hashtag

hi *(exc)* hi

hockey *(nom)* hockey

homage *(nom)* honor

honda *(nom)* motorcycle

hoteli *(nom)* hotel

hydrogen *(sci)* hydrogen

iba *(act)* steal

ibala *(nom)* garden

ibele sin *(nom)* breast

ibila *(act)* sink

ibukisha *(act)* remember

ibuku lya makwebo *(nom)* ledge

ibula *(nom)* leaf

ibutukilo *(nom)* refuge

ibuula *(act)* peel

ica bune *(adj)* fourth

ica cine *(adj)* ideal

ica ibela *(adj)* special

ica ikumi limo na fitatu *(adj)* thirteenth

ica kambatikwa *(adj)* parched

icabeka *(adj)* glossy

icabipa *(adj)* filthy

icabubili *(adj)* second

icabwanga *(adj)* poisonous

icacikulu *(adj)* main

icacine *(adv)* truly

icafuma *(nom)* product

icakosa *(adj)* solid

icakosa *(adj)* hard

icakucita *(nom)* duty

icakucita *(nom)* project

icakufwala *(nom.1)* attire

icakukopelako ifikope *(nom)* camera

icakukushila ifiko *(nom)* dustpan

icakulandilamo *(nom)* microphone

icakulangisha *(nom)* symbol

ichakulya icakulya *(nom)* food

icakulya calu celo *(nom)* breakfast

icakusekesha *(adj)* amusing

ukwishibisha icakwambilapo *(nom)* introduction

icakwambula *(nom)* quotation

icakwishibisha *(nom)* preface

icalenga amakumi yabili *(adj)* twentieth

icalenga cine lubali *(adj)* seventeenth

icalenga ikumi cine konse konse *(adj.1)* eighteenth

icalenga ikumi na fine *(adj)* fourteenth

icalenga ikumilimo nafibili *(adj)* twelfth

icalenga pabula *(adj)* nineteenth

icalo *(nom)* soil

icalo *(nom)* continent

icalo *(nom)* state

icalo *(nom)* universe

icalo cimbi *(adj)* international

icamba *(nom)* marijuana

icamishila *(adj)* striped

icamuselu *(adj)* disgusting

ichani *(nom)* grass

icanso *(nom.1)* weapon

icapwa *(act)* tattered

icashupa *(adj)* difficult

icashupa *(adv)* hard

icashupa *(adj)* tough

icawamisha *(adj)* wonderful

icefya *(adj)* humble

icekumi *(nom)* tithe

icela *(nom.1)* metal

ichinyo *(nom)* vagina

ici *(pro)* this

ici tumbuka *(nom)* Tumbuka

ici unda iciunda *(nom)* sound

icibansa *(nom)* stadium

icibi *(nom.1)* door

icibimbi *(nom)* cucumber

icibombelo *(nom)* tool

icibulukutu *(nom)* thunder

icibumba *(nom.1)* wall

icibusa *(nom)* friendship

icifuba *(nom.1)* chest

icifukushi *(nom)* envy

icifulo *(nom)* position

icifungo *(nom)* prison

icikolopo *(nom)* rag

icikope *(nom)* picture

icikukuma *(nom.1)* quake

icikulwa *(nom)* infrastructure

icikulwa *(nom)* building

icikulwa cabufumu *(nom)* castle

icikulwa cakutambila ifitunshi tunshi *(nom)* theatre

icikunkubiti *(nom)* barrel

icila *(nom)* hammock

icilafi *(nom.1)* forgetfulness

icilaka *(nom.1)* thirst

icilangililo *(nom)* example

icilembelo *(nom.1)* pen

icililo *(nom)* funeral

icilimba *(nom.0)* radio

iciloto *(nom)* dream

icilubo *(nom)* mistake

icimbaya mbaya *(nom)* vehicle

icimfulunganya *(adj)* chaotic

icimfulunganya icimfulunganya *(nom)* confusion

icimonwa *(nom.1)* vision

icimpompo *(nom)* headgear

muti icimuti *(nom)* tree

icinanazi *(nom)* pineapple

icine *(nom)* truth

icineceka *(nom.1)* itself

icinga inchinga *(nom)* bicycle

icinshingwa *(nom.1)* shadow

icintelelwe *(nom)* shade

icipanda *(nom)* goal

icipangano *(nom)* covenant

icipaso *(nom)* grasshopper

icipatala *(nom.1)* clinic

icipe *(nom)* asset

icipe icipe *(nom)* property

icipele *(nom.1)* woodpigeon

icipelebesha *(nom)* butterfly

icipeya *(nom.1)* shoulder

icipinda cakwikalamo *(nom)* living-room

icipingo *(nom.1)* testament

icipowe *(nom)* poverty

icipuku *(nom)* apparition

icipuna *(nom)* chair

icipuna *(nom.1)* bench

umuputule iciputule *(nom)* room

iciputulwa *(nom)* chapter

iciputulwa *(nom)* sector

iciputulwa *(nom)* part

icipyango *(nom)* broom

icisabi *(nom)* porpoise

icisabi *(nom)* whale

icisakulo *(nom)* comb

icisansa ukuboko *(nom)* hand

icishango *(nom.1)* shield

icishibilo *(nom)* sign

icishibilo *(nom)* signpost

icishibilo *(nom)* logo

icishibisho *(nom)* announcement

icishima *(nom)* borehole

icishimu *(nom)* caterpillar

icishininkisho *(nom.1)* proof

icishinka *(adj)* true

icishipwa *(nom.1)* infinity

icishipwa *(adj)* permanent

icisoso ɲamakolo *(nom)* rubbish

icisoso *(nom)* trash

icisoso *(nom)* waste

icisumino *(nom.1)* belief

icisushi *(nom)* fart

icitabo *(nom)* book

icitanga menshi *(nom)* water-melon

kutemwa icitemwiko *(nom)* love

icitende *(nom)* ankle

kutetekela icitetekelo *(nom)* faith

icitofu *(nom)* oven

icitunshi tunshi *(nom.0)* television

iciyongoli *(nom)* centipede

ico *(adv)* therefore

icola *(nom)* bag

icongo *(nom)* noise

iculu catu shishi *(nom)* anthill

icungwa *(nom.1)* orange

icupo *(nom)* marriage

icushi *(nom.1)* smoke

icuuni *(nom)* bird

ifi *(det)* these

ifibashi *(nom)* leprosy

ifiko *(nom)* dirt

ifingi *(adj)* several

ifintu *(nom)* things

ifiseseya *(nom)* ringworm

ifishilingile pakashita *(act)* befit

ifumo *(nom)* stomach

ifumo *(nom.1)* pregnancy

ifunde ifunde *(nom)* advice

ifunde *(nom)* rule

isambililo ifunde *(nom)* lesson

ifupa *(nom)* bone

ifwaku mishi intambi *(nom)* tradition

ifwe *(pro)* we

ifwe *(pro)* us

ifwe fweka *(pro)* ourselves

ifyaku chita ifyakucita *(nom)* solution

ifyakubomfya *(nom.1)* material

ifyakucita *(nom)* activity

ifyakufwala *(nom.1)* clothes

ifyakuwamisha ameno *(nom)* toothpaste

ifyesu *(pro)* ours

igbo *(nom)* Igbo

iikota *(nom)* hen

iipayo mwine *(nom)* suicide

ikala *(act)* settle

ikala *(nom.1)* seat

ikaloti *(nom)* carrot

ikanga *(nom)* guinea-fowl

ikata *(act)* catch

ikata *(act)* grab

ikata *(act)* hold

ikatilila *(act)* have a hold on

ikatisha *(act)* grasp

iketani *(nom.1)* curtain

iko *(pos)* its

ikofi *(nom)* fist

ikonala *(nom)* corner

ikoti *(nom)* coat

ikufi *(nom)* knee

ikumbi *(nom.1)* cloud

ikumi *(adj)* ten

ikumi na bili *(adj)* twelve

ikumi na cine konse konse *(adj)* eighteen

ikumi na cine lubali *(adj)* seventeen

ikumi na mutanda *(adj)* sixteen

ikumi na ne *(adj)* fourteen

ikumi na pabula *(adj)* nineteen

ikumi na sano *(adj)* fifteen

ikumi na tatu *(adj)* thirteen

ikumi na umo *(adj)* eleven

ilaya *(nom)* shirt

ilaya *(nom)* t-shirt

ilaya *(nom)* skirt

ilibwe *(nom)* stone

ilibwe lya pa cifutu *(nom.1)* cornerstone

ilimi *(nom)* Ndebele

ilishanya *(act)* whine

ilonda *(nom)* wasp

iluba *(nom)* flower

ilula *(act)* translate

ilyashi *(nom)* story

ilyo *(adv)* when

ima *(act)* rise

ima *(act)* awaken

imba *(act)* dig

imba *(act)* sing

imbalala *(nom)* groundnut

imbalaminwe *(nom.1)* ring

imbeketi *(nom)* bucket

imbila *(nom)* message

imbila *(nom)* news

imbokoshi *(nom.0)* box

imboyo *(nom.1)* elbow

imbushi *(nom)* goat

imfula *(nom)* rain

imfula yamabwe *(adj)* snowy

imfula yamabwe *(nom)* snow

imfwa *(nom)* death

imfyo *(nom)* kidney

imibele *(nom)* habit

imibele *(nom)* conscience

mibele micitile imibele *(nom)* behaviour

imibele yacine *(adj)* solemn

imibikile *(nom.1)* application

imibombele *(nom)* framework

imibomfeshe *(nom)* usage

imicitile *(nom)* creativity

imikalile *(nom)* lifestyle

imikonkele *(nom)* sequence

imiku *(nom.1)* throughput

imililile yaciunda *(nom)* pitch

imilumbe *(nom)* idiom

imimonekele *(nom)* quality

imimonekele *(nom)* likeness

imimonekele *(nom)* reflection

iminina *(act)* stand

imipangilwe *(nom)* design

imishila *(nom)* stripe

imisomali nɛkɛpuɛnti *(nom)* nail

imisonko umusonko *(nom)* tax

imitantikile *(nom)* programme

imitantikile *(nom)* disposition

impaanga *(nom.1)* sheep

umwina mpalamano *(nom)* neighbourhood

impanga *(nom)* country

impanga *(nom)* bush

impanga *(nom)* forest

impanga *(act)* land

impanga incende *(nom)* land

impanga *(nom.1)* environment

impanga *(nom.1)* lamb

impapa *(nom.1)* leather

impasa *(nom)* mat

impendwa *(nom)* quantity

impiya *(nom.1)* currency

impolo polo *(nom)* bullet

impombo *(nom)* antelope

imwe *(pro)* you

imwe *(pro)* yourselves

imwefu *(nom)* mustache

imya *(act)* lift

imyefu *(nom)* beard

imyendele *(nom.1)* transportation

ina *(adj)* fat

inama *(nom.1)* beef

inama *(nom)* animal

inama *(nom)* meat

inama yankumba lɛ *(nom)* pork

inama yapang'anda *(nom)* pet

incende kɛfɛn *(nom)* constituency

incende *(nom)* territory

incende inchende *(nom)* place

incende *(nom.1)* island

inchende *(nom)* state

inchende ncende *(nom)* space

nchito inchito *(nom)* job

indalama *(nom)* cash

indalama shi tulamo indalama

shifumamo *(nom)* income

indeke *(nom.1)* aeroplane

Indian *(adj)* Indian

indimu *(nom)* lemon

indobo *(nom.1)* fish-hook

indoshi *(nom.1)* wizard

indyato *(nom.1)* slippers

ine *(pro)* me

ine *(pro)* I

ine neka *(pro)* myself

infungulo *(nom.1)* key

ing'anda ing'anda *(nom)* house

ing'anda ya mfumu *(nom)* palace

ing'anda yakusungilamo *(nom)* storehouse

ing'anda yakusungilamo *(nom.1)* warehouse

ing'oma *(nom)* drum

ing'wena *(nom)* alligator pepper

ingi *(adj)* many

ingila *(act)* enter

ingisha *(act)* score

ingisha *(act)* inject

ingisha *(act)* deposit

inkalata *(nom)* Mali

inkalata *(nom)* letter

inkama *(nom)* privacy

inkama *(nom)* secret

inkanda *(nom)* skin

inkasa *(nom.1)* footstep

inkoko *(nom)* chicken

inkola *(nom.1)* snail

inkomaki *(act)* cup

inkonde *(nom)* banana

inkondo ya mitundu *(nom)* civil war

inkongole *(nom)* loan

inkongole *(nom.1)* debt

inkonya *(nom.1)* boxing

inkopyo *(nom.1)* eyelash

inkulo *(nom)* nation

inkunda *(nom)* dove

inkupiko *(nom.1)* lid

insala *(adj)* hungry

insala *(nom)* hunger

insalamu *(nom)* dowry

insalu *(nom)* cloth

insambu *(nom.1)* permission

insamushi *(nom)* maths

insansa *(nom)* pleasure

insansa *(nom)* joy

insapato insapato *(nom)* shoe

insebele *(nom)* deer

insekete *(nom)* jaw

insele *(nom)* insults

insele *(nom.1)* insult

inshila *(nom)* path

inshila *(nom)* way

inshila yakutwala kucilye *(nom)* litigation

inshita *(nom)* moment

inshita *(nom.1)* times

inshita ikesa *(nom)* future

inshita shakale *(nom.1)* ancient times

inshita shakale *(nom.1)* antiquity

inshita ya bumi *(nom.1)* lifetime

inshita yakukabanga *(nom)* East Timor

inshita yalapitapo *(nom)* duration

inshita yamfula *(nom)* wet season

insofu *(nom)* elephant

insoka *(nom)* snake

insoni *(nom)* shyness

insoni *(adj)* shy

intafi intamfu *(nom)* distance

intambo *(nom.1)* rope

intanda *(nom.1)* star

intanda-bwanga *(nom)* tuberculosis

intaneti *(nom.0)* internet

intanshi *(nom)* first

katungulula *(nom.1)* leader

intumba *(nom)* pillar

intungulushi *(nom)* director

inyeleti *(nom.1)* needle

inyeleti *(nom)* syringe

inyenjele *(nom)* bell

inyimbo *(nom)* music

lwimbo inyimbo *(nom)* song

ipalo *(nom)* blessing

ipange *(act)* pretend

ipapao *(nom)* pawpaw

ipaya *(act)* kill

ipeela *(nom.1)* guava

ipekanya *(adv)* ready

ipendo ipendo *(nom)* number

ipendwa ya bantu *(nom)* population

ipenga *(nom.1)* warhorn

ipenga *(nom.1)* trumpet

ipepala *(nom.1)* document

ipepala *(nom)* paper

ipi *(adj)* small

ipika *(act)* cook

ipinda *(nom.2)* proverb

ipindo *(nom.1)* wing

ipipa *(adj)* short

ipulanga *(nom.1)* plank

ipusha *(act)* ask

ipusukilo *(nom)* salvation

isa *(act)* come

isa *(nom.1)* coming

isabi *(nom)* fish

isabi *(nom)* shrimp

isabi *(act)* fish

isabi lyamumatipa *(nom)* mud-fish

Isaki *(din)* Isaac

isala *(act)* block

isala *(nom)* zip

isala *(act)* shut

isala *(act)* close

isali *(nom)* prayer

isambililo *(nom)* topic

isese *(nom)* category

ishiba *(act)* know

ishibikwa *(nom.1)* reputation

ishibisha *(act)* announce

ishibisha *(act)* let ... know

ishina *(nom)* appellation

ishina ishina *(nom.1.4)* name

ishina *(nom)* title

ishina lya *(nom)* noun

ishitima *(act)* train

ishiwi *(nom)* voice

ishiwi *(nom)* word

Islamu *(nom.1)* Islam

Islamu *(adj)* Islamic

isubilo *(nom.1)* confidence

subilo isubilo *(nom)* hope

isula *(adj)* full

isula *(act)* open

isumbu *(nom)* fishing-net

isumbu *(nom)* net

isusha akanwa *(nom)* mouthful

itaba *(nom)* maize

itaila *(nom)* tyre

Italiya *(nom)* Italy

itambula *(nom)* tumbler

itebulo itebulo *(nom)* table

itempele *(nom)* temple

itenti *(nom.1)* tent

itiketi *(nom.1)* ticket

itila *(act)* pour

itoloshi *(nom)* trouser

itoni lyakutusha *(nom)* comma

itontonkanyo *(nom)* thought

Itsekiri *(kw.1)* Itsekiri

ituka *(nom)* shop

itumba *(nom)* wallet

itumba *(nom)* pocket

itungi *(nom)* angle

ivory *(nom)* ivory

iwaicefya *(adj)* royal

iwe *(pro)* you

iwe *(pro)* you

iwe *(pro)* your

iwe *(pro)* you

iyashi lyabumi *(nom.1)* biography

jama *(nom.1)* public

Jamaica *(nom)* Jamaica

jele *(nom)* jail

timu jɛkulu *(nom)* team

jinja *(nom)* ginger

Johannesburg *(din)* Johannesburg

jukɔrɔ *(adv)* under

juru *(act)* loan

ka cɛsiri *(act)* thrive

ka kofɔ *(act)* order

lolekesha ka kɔlɔsi *(nom)* monitor

ka sanbala yɛlɛn *(act)* overgrow

kaba *(adj)* hot

kabasa *(nom)* carpenter

kabeji *(nom.1)* cabbage

Kabengele kakalamba *(nom)* February

Kabengele kanono *(nom)* January

kabepa *(nom)* cheater

kabepa *(nom)* liar

kabika *(nom)* organizer

kabila *(act)* desire

kabinge *(cjn)* nevertheless

kabomba *(nom)* worker

kabungwe *(nom)* society

kacelo *(adj)* early

kacelo celo *(adv)* early

kachimfya *(nom.1)* conqueror

kacita *(nom)* actor

kacita mwanakashi *(nom)* actress

kadi *(nom.1)* card

kadoli *(nom.1)* carton

kafundisha kafundisha *(nom)* teacher

kafwa *(nom)* helper

kafwa *(nom)* sponsor

kafwa *(nom)* hero

kafwilisha wandalama *(nom)* philanthropist

kafya *(adj)* loud

kaka *(act)* tie

kaka *(adv)* not

kakoma wa ng'ombe *(nom)* butcher

kakumba *(nom.1)* pastor

kala *(act)* stay

kalamba *(adj)* serious

kalamba *(adj)* great

kalandila wamilandu *(nom)* lawyer

kalashi *(nom)* class

kalata *(nom.1)* vote

kale *(adj)* ancient

kalemba kaleemba *(nom)* writer

kalefulefu *(nom)* chin

kalekelela *(nom.1)* emancipator

kalemba welyashi *(nom)* journalist

kalenda *(nom)* calendar

kalenga *(nom)* maker

kalenkan *(nom.1)* perjury

mwaiseni *(exc)* welcome

kaling'ongo *(nom)* scorpion

kalipa *(adj)* painful

kalipila *(act)* punish

kalubi *(nom.3)* doll

kalubula *(nom.1)* saviour

kalulu *(nom)* hare

kalulu *(nom)* rabbit

kalumba *(nom)* supporter

kalundwe *(nom)* cassava

kalunga *(nom)* hunter

kalungisha *(nom)* engineer

kama *(act)* squeeze

kamana *(nom)* brook

kambatika *(act)* attach

kambili *(nom)* palmnut

kamfulumende *(nom)* governance

kamfulumende kamfulumende *(nom)* government

kampani kampani *(nom)* company

kampeni kampena *(nom)* campaign

kampu *(nom)* camp

kamukolwe *(nom.1)* cockerel

kana *(act)* reject

kana *(act)* deny

kana cindika *(act)* dishonor

kana totela *(adj)* ungrateful

kanachindika *(act)* dishonour

kandolo *(nom)* sweet potato

kangala *(nom)* athlete

kanyense *(nom.3)* onion

kapanga *(nom)* producer

kapata *(nom)* hater

kapekanya *(nom)* waiter

kapela *(nom)* giver

Kapepo kakalamba *(nom)* June

Kapepo kanono *(nom)* May

kapeti *(nom.0)* carpet

kapinda ka ku kulyo *(adj)* southern

kapinda ka kukuso *(nom)* north

kapinda ka kulyo *(nom.1)* south

kapokola polishi *(nom)* police

kapumpe *(nom)* eagle

kaputula wa milandu *(nom)* judge

Kasakantobo *(nom)* August

kasambilila *(nom.1)* student

kasambilila wamakwebo *(nom.1)* apprentice

kasesema *(nom)* prophet

kashika *(adj)* red

kashita *(nom.1)* customer

kashitisha *(nom.1)* seller

kaso *(nom)* avarice

kastaneti *(nom)* castanet

kasuba kabalika *(adj)* sunny

kasuli *(nom)* lastborn

kasunga wang'anda *(nom)* housekeeper

kasusu *(nom.1)* bat

katapa katapa *(adj)* green

kateka kateka *(nom)* president

katoba wamutima *(nom)* heartbreaker

katungulula *(nom)* chairman

katungulula *(nom)* coach

katungulula *(nom)* master

keke keke *(nom)* cake

kelula *(nom.1)* translator

kemba *(nom)* musician

kemba *(nom.1)* artist

kengisha wa nchito *(nom)* employer

kensha wa bwato *(nom)* helmsman

ubutantinko kɛli *(nom)* procession

kicini *(nom.0)* kitchen

kilomita *(nom.1)* kilometre

kilomita *(nom.1)* kilometer

kobeka *(act)* hang

kocelela wafyela *(nom)* blacksmith

kofi *(nom.1)* coffee

kofi *(din)* Kofi

koini *(nom)* coin

koko *(nom.1)* cocoa

kola *(nom)* cough

kola *(act)* cough

kolani *(nom.1)* koran

kolasi kolasi *(nom)* chorus

kolegi *(nom)* college

kolonganika *(act)* gather

kolwe *(nom)* ape

nsange *(nom)* monkey

kompyuta *(nom)* computer

Kongo *(nom)* Kongo

konka *(act)* follow

konkanyapo *(act)* continue

konkapo *(adj)* next

konse *(pro)* everywhere

kontola *(act)* brake

kopa *(act)* photograph

kosa *(adj)* strong

koselesha *(act)* encourage

kosha *(act)* strengthen

koswe *(nom)* mouse

kote *(adj)* old

krio *(nom.1)* Krio

ku *(pre)* to

ku *(pre)* for

ku *(pre)* by

ku bwaiche *(nom)* childhood

ku kuso *(adj)* left

kubi *(nom.4)* vulture

kucalo *(nom.1)* abroad

kucipinda *(nom)* bedroom

kufyalo *(adj)* western

kukabanga *(nom)* east

kukana ishiba *(adj)* unfamiliar

kula *(act)* build

kula *(act)* grow

kula *(act)* construct

kulamfya *(nom.1)* pollution

kulu *(adj)* big

kulu *(adj)* huge

kulu *(adj)* large

kumabala *(nom)* farm

kumanya *(act)* meet

kumbata *(nom)* hug

kumbinkanya *(nom)* link

kumbinkanya *(act)* integrate

kumbinkanya *(act)* combine

kumbwa *(act)* admire

kumbwisha *(nom)* adulation

kumulu *(nom)* heaven

kumuna *(act)* wipe

kumushi kumwesu *(nom)* home-town

kumya *(act)* touch

senda kungokɔnɔ wulu *(nom)* bear

kungula *(adj)* clear

kunse *(nom)* outdoors

kunse kwa musumba *(nom)* outskirt

kuntanshi *(adv)* forward

kuntashi *(nom)* front

kunuma *(nom)* behind

kunuma *(nom)* rear

kunuma *(pre)* behind

kunuma *(act)* rear

kusa *(act)* fray

kusenamina ulese *(nom)* grace

kushintilila *(adj)* dependable

kushipa *(nom)* courage

kushipikisha *(nom)* patience

kutali *(nom.1)* Afar

kutemwa *(nom)* will

kuti *(adj)* possible

Kutumpu *(nom)* March

kututila ukusungisha *(nom)* investment

kutwi *(nom)* ear

kwakusanga *(nom)* location

kwata *(act)* have

kwata *(nom.1)* possessive

kwindi *(nom)* rat

kwishilya *(nom)* beach

laba *(act)* forget

laboletoli sɛkɛsɛkɛli yɔrɔ *(nom)* laboratory

labu *(nom.1)* lab

labɛn *(act)* made up

lala *(act)* sleep

lamya *(act)* phone

landa *(act)* talk

landa *(act)* speak

landa naya *(act)* say goodbye

langa *(act)* show

Langashe *(nom)* October

langi *(nom)* colour

leta *(act)* bring

leka *(act)* let

leka *(act)* cancel

leka *(act)* stop

lekelela *(act)* free

lekesha *(act)* interrupt

lelo *(adv)* today

lemana *(adj)* disabled

lemba *(act)* write

lemba *(act)* book

lenga *(act)* create

lepula *(act)* tear

Lesa Lesa *(nom.1)* God

levi *(nom)* levy

libili libili *(adv)* often

libu *(nom.1)* liver

libwe *(nom)* rock

Libya *(nom)* Libya

Likpakpaln *(nom.1)* Konkomba

lila *(act)* cry

lilya *(adv)* then

limbi *(adv)* maybe

limbi *(adv)* later

limbula *(act)* pluck

limo limofye *(adv)* seldomly

linda *(act)* guard

linga *(adj)* adequate

linganya *(pre)* just

lini *(nom)* egg

linkolobwe *(adj)* orange

lino *(nom.4)* tooth

linso *(nom)* eye

lipila *(act)* pay

lipoti *(nom)* report

lithium *(sci.1)* lithium

lithuania *(nom)* Lithuania

lolesha *(act)* look

Lomwe *(nom.1)* Lomwe

londolola *(act)* explain

londolola ubulondoloshi *(nom)* explanation

londoloshi *(adj)* descriptive

London *(nom.1)* London

longololo lwa numa *(nom.1)* spine

losha *(act)* mean

lota *(act)* dream

lowa *(adj)* sweet

lubalala *(nom)* nut

lubelo *(nom)* razor

lubembu *(nom)* sin

lubilo *(adj)* fast

lubilo *(nom)* speed

lubuka *(adj)* free

lubulula *(nom)* accounts

lubuto *(nom)* seed

lufya *(act)* lose

lufyengo *(adj)* wrong

luka *(act)* braid

lumbanya *(act)* praise

lumbuka *(adj)* distinguished

lumbula *(act)* mention

lunda *(act)* increase

lundapo *(nom)* adjective

lundinkanya *(act)* join

lungama *(adj)* straight

lungamika *(adj)* right

lungisha *(act)* repair

lunshi *(nom)* housefly

lupili *(nom)* hill

lupwa *(nom)* sibling

luse masiban *(nom)* grief

luse *(nom.1)* remorse

luse luse *(adj)* pitiful

lusengo *(nom.1)* horn

lusuba *(nom)* summer

Lusuba lunono *(nom)* September

lutombo *(nom)* bud

lutungu *(nom)* hip

lwa *(act)* fight

lwala *(adj)* sick

lya *(act)* eat

lyonse *(adv)* daily

lyonse *(adv)* always

ma *(act)* beat

ukubomfya nengu ma kɔlɔsili *(nom)* espionage

maa *(nom)* Maasai

macini *(nom)* machine

mafisa kanwa *(nom)* bribery

mafisa kanwa *(nom.1)* bribe

mafupa mafupa *(nom)* skeleton

mafuta *(nom)* oil

magazini *(nom)* magazine

mailo *(adv)* yesterday

mailo *(adv)* tomorrow

maka *(nom)* vitality

maka *(nom.1)* effort

maka *(nom)* energy

maka maka *(adj)* energetic

makanta *(nom)* locust

Mako *(nom)* mark

makumbi makumbi *(adj)* blue

makumi cine konse konse *(adj)* eighty

makumi cine lubali *(adj)* seventy

makumi mutanda *(adj)* sixty

makumi pabula *(adj)* ninety

makumi yane *(adj)* forty

makumi yasano *(adj)* fifty

makumi yatatu *(adj)* thirty

malaiti *(adj)* electronic

malaria *(nom)* malaria

malilo *(nom)* wailing

malinso *(nom)* gecko

malumbo *(nom)* praise

maluti *(nom.1)* gunpowder

mango mango *(nom)* mango

mano *(adj)* wise

mano uwamano *(adj)* intelligent

mano *(nom)* wisdom

mano *(adj)* mental

mapu *(nom)* map

masa *(nom)* plaster

mfumu masakɛ *(nom)* king

masalula *(nom)* scorn

masamba *(nom)* west

mashindano *(nom)* exam

mask *(nom.1)* mask

Mateo *(nom.1)* Matthew

mayo *(nom)* mom

mayo mayo *(nom)* mum

mayosenge tɛnɛmuso *(nom)* aunty

mbale *(nom)* plate

mbale *(nom.1)* bowl

mbata *(nom)* duck

mbeketi *(nom)* pail

mbelela uluse *(exc)* excuse me

mboni *(nom.1)* witness

mbwa *(nom)* dog

mbwili *(nom)* leopard

mchinsi *(nom)* honour

meloni *(nom)* melon

membala *(nom)* member

metaphor *(nom.1)* metaphor

mfimfi *(nom.1)* darkness

mfumu *(nom)* chieftain

mfumu *(nom.1)* chief

mfuti *(nom)* gun

mfwa *(act)* hear

mfwalashi *(nom)* horse

mibele *(nom)* manner

mibele *(nom.1)* custom

mibele *(nom.1)* culture

mibombele *(nom.1)* management

micitile *(nom)* action

micitile *(act)* act

milandu ya kale *(nom)* history

milangwe *(adj)* funny

milioni *(adj)* million

miloshi *(nom)* mile

mina *(act)* swallow

mineti *(nom)* minute

misepela inono *(nom)* teenager

mishila *(nom.1)* root

mo fye *(nom)* singleton

mona *(act)* see

mosiki *(nom)* mosque

motoka *(nom)* taxi

motoka *(nom.2)* car

motoka *(nom)* van

mpalamano mpalamano *(nom)* neighbour

mpanga *(adj)* wild

mpela *(nom)* end

mpepa *(act)* pray

mpepo *(nom)* fever

mpilipili mpilipili mpilipili *(nom)* pepper

mpundu *(nom.1)* twin

mpunga *(nom)* grain

mpusho *(nom)* unit

msango *(nom)* character

mu *(pre)* in

mu kalashi *(nom)* classroom

mubili *(nom.1)* body

mubwingi *(adj)* plenty

mubwingi *(act)* retail

mubwingi *(adj)* plural

mucele *(nom)* salt

mucence *(nom)* parrot

mucila *(nom)* tail

mucilye *(nom)* court

tasha mucinshi *(nom)* gratitude

mufumbi *(adj)* rainy

mufyala *(nom)* cousin

muka mfwilwa *(nom)* widower

mukalamba *(nom)* adult

mukalamba *(nom.1)* elder

mukamfwilwa *(nom)* widow

mukashana *(nom)* girl

mukati *(pre)* inside

mukolamfula *(nom)* rainbow

mukonko umupoka poka *(nom)* valley

mukoshi *(nom.2)* neck

mukunso *(nom.2)* leg

mukwai *(nom.1)* sir

mukwai *(adv)* please

mukwapa *(nom)* armpit

mulale bwino *(exc)* sleep tight

mulambo *(nom)* tribute

mulandu *(nom)* purpose

mulandu *(nom)* affair

mulandu *(nom.1)* crime

mulandu mulandu *(nom)* reason

muleshi *(nom)* nurse

mulilo *(nom.1)* fire

mulimi *(nom.1)* farmer

mulimo *(nom)* use

mulinso *(nom)* lizard

mulongo *(act)* row

mulongo *(nom)* row

mulu *(nom)* sky

mulumbe *(nom.1)* fable

mulume *(nom)* husband

mulumendo *(nom.1)* boy

mulwani *(nom.1)* enemy

mumana *(nom)* stream

mumbu *(nom)* yam

mumpempo *(nom)* winter

mumu bwekesha *(nom)* feedback

munda *(nom.1)* womb

mung'wi ng'wi *(nom)* mosquito

muntontonkanya *(nom)* idea

muntu *(adj)* human

muntu *(nom.1)* person

muntu muntu *(nom)* human

munyina *(nom)* brother

mupina *(adj)* poor

Mupundu-milimo *(nom)* December

umupunga mupunge *(nom)* rice

musalu *(nom)* lettuce

musalula *(act)* abuse

musango *(act)* type

musango *(nom)* type

musango *(nom)* structure

musango *(adj)* kind

musao *(nom.1)* cushion

musao musao *(nom)* pillow

musebo *(nom)* road

museke museke *(nom)* basket

musepela *(nom)* youth

mushika *(nom)* manager

mushilika *(nom)* soldier

mushilo *(adj)* holy

mushipa wa mulopa *(nom.1)* vein

umwanakashi musoma *(nom)* female

musonkano ɲɔnkunbɛ *(nom)* conference

musonkano *(nom)* event

musuma suma *(adj.1)* good

musumba *(nom)* capital

musunga *(act)* paste

mutanda *(adj)* sixth

mutanda *(adj)* six

mutemwikwa *(nom)* dear

mutende *(nom)* health

mutengo *(nom)* price

mutengo *(nom.1)* wood

mutengo mutengo *(nom)* value

mutima *(nom)* heart

mutima usuma *(nom.1)* sweet-heart

mutoto *(nom.2)* navel

mutungu *(nom)* ox

muyayaya *(adj)* eternal

mwabomba bwino *(exc)* good job

mwabombenipo *(exc)* well done

mwaka umwaka *(nom)* year

mwaloshenipo *(exc)* condolences

mwamfuli *(nom.1)* umbrella

mwana *(nom)* daughter

mwanda *(adj)* hundred

mwankole *(nom)* crow

mwele *(nom)* knife

mwenamo *(nom)* profit

mwende bwino *(exc)* godspeed

mweni *(nom)* stranger

mwentula *(act)* smile

Mwenye *(nom)* Indian

mweshi *(nom)* month

mwina mwandi *(nom.1)* spouse

mwina obe umwina mobe *(nom)* partner

mwinga *(nom.1)* concubine

mwisaisa *(nom)* immigrant

mwishikulu *(nom)* nephew

myaka *(nom.1)* age

myanga *(act)* lick

na *(cjn)* and

na *(cjn)* with

na *(adv)* and

na nomba *(adv)* still

nabwinga *(nom)* bride

nakaana *(exc)* sorry

nakabili *(adv)* also

nakabumba *(nom)* porter

nako mutengo *(adj)* cheap

nakufuluka *(exc)* i miss you

nakuka *(adj)* weak

nakulu *(nom)* grandmother

nang'ana *(adj)* soft

nang'ani *(adj)* boring

nang'ani *(adj)* lazy

nani *(pro)* who

nasali *(nom.1)* nursery

nasenge *(nom)* auntie

natotela *(exc)* thanks

natotela *(exc)* thank you

naya *(nom)* bye

nchende *(nom)* venue

nchusha *(nom.1)* bother

ndalama *(nom)* money

ndifye bwino *(exc)* I am well

ndupi *(nom)* palm

ndusha *(nom)* bile

ndusha *(nom)* gall

ndyabuluba ndyabuluba *(nom)* giraffe

ne *(adj)* four

nekileshi *(nom.1)* necklace

nengu *(nom.1)* spy

network *(nom.1)* network

ng'ombe *(nom)* cow

nga *(pre)* like

nga ..., *(cjn)* if ... then

ngamali *(nom)* camel

ngashi *(nom)* coconut

ngoshe *(nom)* python

ngw'ena *(nom)* alligator

ngwena *(nom)* crocodile

nina *(adv)* up

nina *(act)* climb

ninshi *(adv)* why

nkafi *(nom)* paddle

nkalamo *(nom)* lion

nkalata *(nom)* mail

nkashi *(nom.1)* sister

nkasu *(nom)* robe

nkoko *(nom.1)* fowl

nkoloko *(nom)* clock

nkolokoso nkolokoso *(nom)* wrist

nkonde shaipikwa *(nom)* plantain

nkondo *(nom.1)* war

nkonko *(adj)* pure

nkumba *(nom)* pig

nkumba inya *(nom.1)* piglet

nkuni *(nom)* firewood

nkupiko *(nom)* cover

nomba *(adv)* now

nomba *(adj)* just

nombaline *(adv)* immediately

nondo *(nom)* hammer

nonka *(adj)* rich

nono *(adv)* a little

nsa *(nom)* hour

nsa *(nom)* wee hours

nsamba *(nom.2)* Iguana

nsambu *(nom.1)* rights

nsansa *(adj)* delightful

nseko *(nom.1)* joke

nshi *(pro)* what

nshi *(det)* which

nshita *(nom)* period

nshita *(nom)* time

nsupa *(nom.1)* calabash

ntambo *(nom.1)* string

ntanshi *(adj)* first

ntendekelo *(nom)* Genesis

ntongwe *(nom)* pea

ntu *(nom)* being

ntulo *(nom)* source

numa *(nom)* back

nunkila *(adj)* fragrant

nunko bubi *(act)* stink

nunshya *(act)* smell

nwa *(act)* drink

nya icisushi *(act)* fart

nya icisushi *(act)* flatulate

nyunsuluka *(adj)* elastic

ɲanki *(act)* blame

ubufi ŋalo *(nom)* lie

obe *(pos)* your

oca *(act)* burn

oca *(act)* roast

ofeshi *(nom.0)* office

ololoka *(adj)* upright

Olomo *(kw)* Oromo

onaula *(act)* ruin

onaula *(act)* spoil

onaula *(act)* sabotage

onda *(adj)* slim

onda *(adj)* thin

ongola *(nom)* influence

onse *(adj)* each

onse *(adj)* any

onse *(adj)* every

onse *(pro)* all

owa *(act)* swim

owe *(act)* owe

pa *(pre)* on

pa *(pre)* at

pa *(nom.1)* point

Pa Cibelushi *(nom)* Saturday

Pa Mulungu *(nom)* Sunday

pa nshita inono *(adv)* soon

pabula *(adj)* nine

padiloko *(nom.1)* padlock

pafu ada *(nom)* puff-adder

pai *(nom)* pie

pakati ukuba pakati *(nom)* fairness

pakati *(nom)* centre

pakati *(nom)* half

pakati *(nom)* middle

pakati ka siphia *(nom)* hemisphere

paki *(nom.1)* park

pakulekelesha *(adj)* last

pakusalwila *(nom)* saucepan

pakuti *(det)* that

pala *(act)* bless

palafini *(nom)* kerosene

Pali Cibili pali cibili *(nom)* Tuesday

Pali Cimo pali cimo *(nom)* Monday

Pali Cine *(nom)* Thursday

Pali Cisano *(nom)* Friday

Pali Citatu *(nom)* Wednesday

palwa *(pre)* about

pama *(adj)* brave

pamaka *(nom)* force

pamala *(nom)* abdomen

pamo *(adj)* total

pamo *(nom.1)* sum

pamo *(nom)* group

pamo *(adv)* together

pamulandu *(nom.1)* account

pamulu *(pre)* above

panda mano *(act)* advise

panga *(act)* plan

panga *(act)* make

panga *(nom)* cast

pani *(nom)* pan

pano *(adv)* here

pano pano *(nom)* here

panse *(adv)* outside

panse *(nom)* outside

panshi *(adv)* down

panshi *(nom)* floor

panshi *(adv)* downward

pantu *(cjn)* because

papata *(act)* beg

papatala *(adj)* flat

parliament *(nom.1)* parliament

parliamentarian *(nom)* parliamentarian

pasifiki *(adj)* Pacific

pasili *(nom)* parsley

pata *(act)* hate

patikisha *(act)* force

peela *(act)* give

pekanya *(nom)* preparation

pekanya *(act)* prepare

pela *(adj)* maximum

pela *(nom)* service

pema *(act)* breathe

pema *(act)* sigh

pembela *(act)* wait

pensulo *(nom.0)* pencil

penta *(act)* paint

penta *(act)* colour

pentagoni *(nom.1)* pentagon

pepi *(adv)* near

pepi pepi *(adv)* quite

pepo *(adj)* purple

pesamba *(pre)* under

petamika *(act)* fold

pikoko *(nom)* peacock

pilibuka *(act)* repent

pima *(act)* weigh

pima *(act)* measure

pimpila *(adj)* annoying

pimpo *(nom)* pimple

pindo muntu *(act)* sue

pinki *(adj)* pink

pita *(act)* cross

pita *(act)* pass

pita *(act)* flow

pito *(nom)* pito

planeti *(nom.0)* planet

plasitiki *(adj)* plastic

poka *(act)* claim

pokelela *(act)* receive

polegi *(nom.1)* porridge

ponya *(act)* drop

Portuguese *(nom.9)* Portuguese

posha *(nom)* greeting

posha *(act)* greet

posha *(act)* heal

potty *(nom)* potty

PPE *(nom.1)* personal protective equipment

printa *(act)* print

pronouni *(nom)* pronoun

pukuta *(act)* scrub

pulinta *(nom)* printer

punda *(act)* shout

punda *(nom)* donkey

pungwa *(act)* hawk

pungwa *(nom)* hawk

Punjabi *(nom.1)* Panjabi

pupuka *(act)* fly

pupuka *(nom)* fly

pusa *(act)* miss

pusanya *(adj)* different

pusene *(nom)* opposite

pusuka *(adj)* safe

pususha *(act)* save

pususha *(act)* rescue

puta *(act)* blow

putaula *(act)* slice

putula *(act)* deduct

putula *(act)* branch

putula *(act)* cut

pwa *(act)* finish

pwa *(act)* end

pwa *(act)* achieve

pwapwa *(nom)* lung

pwisha ukupwisha *(nom)* graduate

pwisha *(act)* deplete

pwisha *(act)* fulfill

pwisha *(act)* spend

repu *(nom.1)* rape

roketi *(nom.0)* rocket

saana *(nom)* lot

saana *(adv)* very

saana fye *(adv)* very much

saana fye *(nom)* conjunction

saca *(nom)* truck

sakamana *(act)* care

sakamana *(nom.1)* worry

sakamana *(nom)* responsibility

sala *(act)* decide

sala *(act)* choose

sala *(nom)* option

sala *(act)* select

saladi *(nom)* salad

salanganya *(act)* scatter

salanganya *(act)* spread

samba *(act)* shower

sambilila *(act)* learn

sambilila *(act)* study

sambilila *(nom.1)* learning

sanga *(act)* found

sanga *(act)* find

sangalala *(adj)* merry

sangalala *(adj)* fun

sangalala *(nom)* happiness

sangula *(act)* change

sangula *(act)* transform

sanitaiza *(nom.1)* sanitizer

sankanya *(act)* mix

sano *(adj)* five

sansabika *(nom)* pride

sansabika *(act)* dignify

sansabika *(act)* exult

sansamuka *(act)* rejoice

sanshya *(act)* add

sasa *(nom)* acid

sashile *(adj)* acidic

sasuka *(act)* yell

satifiketi *(nom)* degree

sausandi *(adj)* thousands

scrape *(act)* scrape

sebana *(act)* shame

seka *(act)* laugh

sekelela *(act)* enjoy

sela *(act)* move

selo *(nom)* cell

sementi *(nom.1)* cement

senda *(act)* carry

senda *(act)* collect

senda *(act)* get

senda *(nom)* pick

shala *(act)* remain

shalapo *(exc)* goodbye

shamfumu shimucindikwa *(nom)* Lord

shana *(act)* dance

shani *(exc)* hello

shatemwikwa *(adj)* undesir-able

sheta *(act)* chew

shi tima *(nom)* ship

shibuka *(act)* wake up

shibwinga *(nom)* groom

shikulu *(nom)* grandpa

shilili *(adj)* silent

shimakwebo *(nom)* trader

shimapepo *(nom)* priest

shimike *(nom)* courtship

shimikila *(act)* preach

shimucindikwa *(nom)* chair-person

shimucindikwa mwanakashi *(nom)* chairwoman

shimya *(act)* switch off

shimya *(act)* turn off

shimya *(act)* extinguish

Shinde *(nom)* April

shindika *(act)* see ... off

shinga *(adj)* how much

shingashinga *(adj)* slow

shinshimuna *(act)* worship

shipula *(act)* doze

shisala *(nom)* scissors

shita *(act)* buy

shitima *(nom.4)* train

shitisha *(act)* sell

shonaula *(act)* grind

shuga *(nom)* sugar

shuka *(adj)* lucky

shunguluka *(act)* surround

shunguluka *(nom)* circle

shupikwa *(nom)* challenge

sikana *(nom)* scanner

siluva *(nom.1)* silver

sing-jama *(act)* sing jama

sipana *(nom)* spanner

siteya *(nom.1)* stair

skuta *(nom)* scooter

so *(nom.1)* saw

sokolola *(act)* reveal

sokoshi *(nom.0)* sock

solwesolwe *(nom)* pioneer

soma *(nom.1)* study

sondolola *(nom.1)* conclusion

songola *(act)* sharpen

songoloka *(adj)* liquid

songoloka *(nom)* liquid

sonkola *(act)* poke

sopo *(nom.0)* soap

sosa *(act)* say

Soto *(nom.1)* Sotho

spatula *(nom)* spatula

sukulu *(nom.0)* school

suma *(nom)* good

suma sana *(adj)* excellent

sumina *(act)* accept

sumina *(act)* agree

suminisha *(act)* allow

suminisha *(act)* approve

sunga *(act)* protect

sunga *(act)* preserve

sunga *(act)* record

sunga *(nom.1)* saving

sunga bwino *(act)* value

sungila *(act)* memorize

sungilila *(act)* maintain

sungusha *(nom.1)* surprise

sunka *(act)* push

sunkana *(act)* tremble

sunkunsha *(act)* shake

Suomi *(nom.1)* Finnish

supuni *(nom.0)* spoon

supuni *(nom)* ladle

supuni iitali *(act)* ladle

suti *(nom)* suit

sutikesi *(nom.1)* suitcase

ta *(pro)* it

tabuleti *(nom)* tablet

tai *(nom.1)* tie

taiga *(nom)* tiger

tailoshi *(nom.1)* tile

talalika *(act)* calm

talalika *(act)* comfort

talalika umutima *(nom)* comfort

talantula *(nom)* tarantula

tali *(adj)* long

tali *(adj)* deep

taluka *(act)* avoid

taluka *(act)* prevent

tamba *(nom)* watch

tamba *(act)* watch

tamfya *(act)* chase

tampula *(act)* step

tamuli *(nom)* nothing

tandabube *(nom.4)* spider

tandala *(act)* visit

tangisha *(adj)* advance

tankile *(nom.1)* order

Tanzania *(nom)* Tanzania

tata *(nom.1)* father

tata wacibili *(nom)* stepfather

tatafyala *(nom)* father-in-law

teka *(act)* govern

telapi *(nom)* therapy

telelesha *(act)* smoothen

telesikopi *(nom)* telescope

temwa *(act)* like

temwa *(act)* love

temwa *(act)* adore

temwa *(nom.1)* content

tentemba *(act)* treat

tesemuna *(act)* sneeze

tesha *(act)* understand

teta *(nom)* sighing

ti *(nom.1)* tea

tikamika *(act)* thicken

tikamika *(adj)* freezing

tilafiki *(nom)* traffic

tililioni *(adj)* trillion

tina *(act)* fear

tina *(act)* wring

tininka *(act)* press

tinta *(act)* pull

tinya *(act)* scare

tinya *(nom)* threat

tinya *(adj)* frightening

tinya *(adj)* scary

tipa *(act)* curse

tishu *(nom.1)* toilet roll

Tito *(nom.1)* Titus

toba *(act)* smash

toba *(act)* break

tofi *(nom.1)* toffee

toloka *(act)* jump

tomato tomato *(nom.0.1)* tomato

tombola *(act)* bud

tomona *(act)* kiss

tondolo *(adj)* quiet

tontonkanya *(act)* think

tontonkanya *(nom.1)* thinking

tota *(act)* clap

totela *(act)* thank

totela *(nom)* thanks

totela *(act)* appreciate

tuma *(act)* send

tumika *(act)* serve

tumpa *(adj)* stupid

tungulula *(act)* reign

tungulula *(nom)* guide

tungulula *(act)* guide

tungulula *(act)* lead

tuntulu *(adj)* entire

turpentine *(nom)* turpentine

tusha *(act)* rest

tutuma *(act)* stumble

twala *(nom)* supply

twala *(act)* take

twalilila pa nshita itali *(adj)* chronic

Twi *(nom)* Twi

twishika *(act)* doubt

ubongo *(nom.1)* brain

ubongo *(nom)* mind

ubowa *(nom)* mushroom

ububi *(nom.1)* wickedness

ubucingo *(nom)* safety

ubucingo ubucingo *(nom)* security

ubufi *(act)* lie

ubufumu *(nom)* throne

ubufumu ubufumu *(nom)* kingdom

ubufumu *(nom)* realm

ubufyashi *(act)* parent

ubukala *(nom)* penis

ubukwebo *(act)* trade

ubulangeti *(nom)* blanket

ubulendo *(nom)* journey

ubulondoloshi *(nom.1)* definition

ubulondoloshi *(nom)* description

ubulwele *(nom)* disease

ubulwele *(nom.1)* illness

ubulwi *(act)* battle

ubulwi *(nom.1)* battle

ubumfisolo *(adj)* secret

ubumi butali *(nom)* longevity

ubumi bwapamulu *(nom)* high-life

ubunang'ani ubunang'ani *(nom)* laziness

ubunonshi *(nom)* trade

ubuntungwa *(nom)* freedom

ubupilibulo ubupilibulo *(nom)*

meaning

ukusala ubupingulo *(nom)* decision

ubupingushi bwayana *(nom)* justice

ubupupu *(nom.1)* theft

ubupyani *(nom.1)* inheritance

ubusaka *(act)* tidy

ubusaka *(nom.1)* cleanliness

ubusanshi *(nom)* bed

ubusansi *(nom)* mattress

ubusanso *(adj)* dangerous

ubusanso *(nom)* accident

ubushiku *(nom)* day

ubushiku bwakufyalwa *(nom.1)* birthday

ubushiku bwakufyalwa *(exc)* happy birthday

ubusuma *(nom)* goodness

ubutali *(adj)* tall

ubutani *(nom.1)* stinginess

ubutungulushi *(nom.1)* leadership

ubwafya *(nom)* issue

ubwafya *(nom)* problem

ubwalwa *(nom)* liquor

ubwalwa *(nom)* alcohol

ubwana *(nom)* adoption

ubwato *(nom)* canoe

ubwato *(nom)* boat

ubwikashi *(nom)* habitat

ubwina kalale *(nom)* urbanism

uko *(nom)* there

uko *(adv)* where

uko utuni tulala *(act)* roost

ukonaula *(nom)* sabotage

ukonaula *(nom)* louse

ukonaula *(nom.1)* spending

ukonaula fimo *(act)* incinerate

uku belenga ukubelenga *(nom)* reading

uku cusha *(nom)* bully

uku cushiwa *(act)* torment

uku ibela *(adj)* unique

uku kwata icisabo *(act)* bear fruit

uku pitamo *(nom)* experience

uku senteka *(act)* bully

uku sunga *(nom)* protection

ukuba *(act)* become

ukuba bwino *(nom)* wellbeing

ukubepesha *(nom.1)* accusation

ukubipa *(adj)* wicked

ukuboko *(nom)* arm

ukubola *(nom)* decay

ukubomfya kompyuta *(nom)* computing

ukubuka *(nom)* resurrection

ukubulungana *(nom)* sex

ukubwela kwa mwaka *(exc)* Year of Return

ukubwesha *(act)* adjust

ukubwesha *(act)* respond

ukuca *(adj)* creative

ukucena *(nom)* prejudice

ukucepa *(nom.1)* scarcity

ukucila *(cjn)* than

ukucimfyanya *(nom)* competition

ukucindikwa *(nom)* dignity

ukucula *(nom)* suffering

ukufulunganya *(nom)* puzzle

ukufulwa *(nom)* anger

ukufulwa *(nom)* aggression

ukufuma *(pre)* from

ukufuma umulopa *(nom)* bleeding

ukufumya *(nom)* subtraction

ukufwaya *(nom)* surf

ukufwaya *(nom.1)* proposal

ukufwaya *(act)* ask ... out

ukufwilwa *(adj)* widowed

ukufwisa amate *(nom)* spittle

ukufyalwa kwamwana *(nom)* childbirth

ukuicefya *(nom)* humility

ukuilanga *(adj)* ostentatious

ukukaba *(nom)* heat

ukukaba kwacalo *(nom)* global warming

ukukaba sakamana *(act)* caress

ukukabila *(nom)* interest

ukukabushanya *(nom)* trading

ukukalipa kwa mutwe *(nom.1)* headache

ukukalipwa *(nom.1)* pain

ukukalipwa mumala *(nom.1)* stomach-ache

ukukana kwata amano *(nom)* nonsense

ukukana kwata ukumfwa *(nom)* apathy

ukukana kwata umufundo *(adj)* infertile

ukukana umfwila *(nom.1)* rebellion

ukukanatotela *(nom)* ingratitude

ukukanya *(act)* disgrace

ukukashika kwelinso *(nom)* conjunctivitis

ukukopa *(nom)* photograph

ukukula *(nom)* growth

ukukumana *(nom)* meeting

ukukumana *(nom)* summit

ukukumba *(act)* steer

ukukumba *(act)* stir

ukukwanisha *(act)* be fitting

ukukwanisha *(nom.1)* achievement

ukukwanisha uku *(act)* be able to

ukukwata *(act)* consist

ukukwata *(pro)* having

ukulaka *(nom)* argument

ukulaka *(nom)* squabbles

ukulaka *(nom)* quarrel

ukulanshanya *(nom.1)* communication

ukulanshanya *(nom)* conversation

ukulapa *(nom)* rap

ukulekana *(nom)* divorce

ukulemba *(nom.1)* writing

ukulembesha *(nom.1)* registration

ukulenga *(nom)* drawing

ukulenga ukulenga *(nom)* creation

ukulenga *(nom.1)* impact

ukulu *(nom.1)* foot

ukulufyanya *(nom)* contempt

ukulumbanisha *(act)* commend

ukulundinkanya *(nom)* connection

ukulunduluka *(nom)* success

ukulwala kwakuluka *(nom)* nausea

ukulya *(act)* dine

ukulya lubilo lubilo *(act)* devour

ukumfwa *(nom)* earring

ukumfwa *(nom.1)* feeling

ukumfwa ububi *(nom)* enmity

ukumfwa ububi *(nom.1)* stress

ukumfwisha bwino *(act)* kindle

ukumfwisha ububi *(act)* annoy

ukumona ifyakuntanshi *(act)* foresee

ukumyanga *(act)* suck

ukunaka *(nom)* fatigue

ukunaka *(nom)* tiredness

ukunasha *(act)* soften

ukundapa *(nom)* healing

ukununkila *(nom)* fragrance

ukununkila *(nom.1)* aesthetic

ukunya *(act)* shit

ukunya *(act)* defecate

ukupalanya *(adj)* familiar

ukupatula *(nom.1)* division

ukupekanya *(nom)* preparations

ukupela ubukata *(act)* glorify

ukupema *(nom)* breath

ukupilibuka *(nom)* repentance

ukupilibula *(nom.1)* change

ukupoleka *(act)* explode

ukuposa *(act)* throw

ukuposa *(nom)* dump

ukuposha *(nom)* salutation

ukupundisha *(act)* scream

ukupwa *(act)* fade

ukupwa kwamulungu *(nom)* weekend

ukupwililika *(adj)* perfect

ukupyanika *(nom.1)* replacement

ukusala ukusala *(nom)* election

ukusambilila *(nom)* schooling

ukusansabika *(nom)* exultation

ukusanshishe *(nom)* collection

ukusefya *(nom)* festival

ukusefya *(nom)* party

ukusenteka *(nom)* sarcasm

ukushana *(nom)* dancing

ukushipa *(nom.1)* virtue

ukushipula shipula *(nom)* drowsiness

ukushita *(act)* purchase

ukushita *(nom.1)* shopping

ukushitisha *(act)* auction

ukushupikwa ukulolekesha *(nom)* peer

ukusoka *(nom.1)* warning

ukusuminisha *(nom)* tolerance

ukusuminisha *(nom)* acceptance

ukusuminishanya *(nom.1)* agreement

ukusunda *(act)* urinate

ukusunga *(act)* keep

ukusunga *(nom)* store

ukusunga *(nom)* preservation

ukusupikwa *(nom)* oppression

ukusupula *(nom)* summarisation

ukutalala *(adj)* cold

ukutalalikwa *(adj)* comfortable

ukutalunkana kwacintu bwingi *(nom.1)* social distancing

ukutampa *(nom)* novice

ukuti *(cjn)* that

ukutina *(nom)* fear

ukutontokanya *(act)* pound

ukutula kwakasuba *(nom)* sunrise

ukutumpa *(nom)* foolishness

ukutungwa *(nom)* injection

ukututuma *(nom.1)* trembling

ukutwala *(nom)* delivery

ukuwaya waya *(nom)* procrastination

ukuya *(nom)* heading

ukwafwa *(nom)* favoritism

ukwakanya *(act)* divide

ukwangufyanya *(adj)* quick

ukwelela *(act)* forgive

ukwenda *(nom)* travel

ukwenda *(nom)* tour

ukwi shibisha *(nom)* information

ukwikala *(adj)* living

ukwikala bwino *(nom)* luxury

ukwikala mukati *(nom.1)* lockdown

ukwikata pamaka *(act)* rape

ukwikatana *(nom)* unity

ukwikatila pamaka *(act)* defile

ukwiluka *(nom)* comprehension

ukwilula ukwilula *(nom)* translation

ukwima *(nom)* raisin

ukwimba *(nom)* singing

ukwimya *(act)* revive

ukwimya *(nom)* lift

ukwingisha *(nom.1)* inclusion

ukwipaya *(nom.1)* murder

ukwishiba shani *(nom)* technology

ulishani *(exc)* how are you

ulubali *(nom)* side

ulubansa *(nom)* yard

ulubuto *(nom)* light

ulucelopo mukwai *(exc)* good morning

ulukasu *(nom)* hoe

ulukobo *(nom)* back of the head

ulukombo *(nom)* cup

ulukungu *(nom)* dust

ululimi ululimi *(nom)* language

ululimi ululimi *(nom)* tongue

ululimi *(nom)* Ururimi

ulupato *(nom)* hatred

ulupemfu *(nom)* cockroach

ulupi *(act)* spank

ulupili *(nom.3)* mountain

ulupwa ulupwa *(nom)* family

uluse *(nom)* empathy

uluse *(nom)* mercy

uluse *(nom)* kindness

uluseko *(nom)* laughter

ulushimu *(nom.1)* bee

ulwala *(nom)* fingernail

ulwambo *(nom)* gossip

uma *(nom)* beat

uma *(act)* hit

uma *(adj)* dry

umbilicus *(nom)* umbilicus

umfwa *(act)* listen

umfwa *(act)* feel

umfwa insoni *(act)* be shy

umfwila *(act)* obey

umika *(act)* dry

umo *(pro)* someone

umo *(adj)* one

umoona *(nom)* nose

umu lwele *(adj)* patient

umubomfi *(nom)* employee

umucanga *(nom.1)* sand

umucila *(act)* tail

umucinshi *(nom)* respect

umufula *(nom.1)* foundation

umufundo *(adj)* fertile

umufundo *(nom.1)* fertility

umufwi *(nom)* arrow

umufwi *(nom.1)* spear

umufyashi *(nom.1)* parent

umukaka *(nom.2)* milk

umukalamba wanchito *(nom)* boss

umukashi *(nom)* wife

umukate umukate *(nom)* bread

umukwapu *(nom)* whip

umulaini *(nom)* line

umulanda *(nom)* indigent

umulomo *(nom)* lip

umulondo *(nom)* fisherman

umulopa *(nom.1)* blood

umulumbe *(nom)* parable

umulungu *(nom.1)* week

umulwelwe *(nom)* patient

umunana *(nom)* river

umunandi umwanakashi *(nom)* girlfriend

umungeli *(nom)* angel

umunobe *(act)* mate

umunono *(adj)* teenage

umunteku nteku *(nom)* hiccups

umuntu *(nom.1)* man

umuntungwa *(nom)* humankind

umupaka *(nom.1)* boundary

umupamba *(nom)* abomination

umupashi umupashi *(nom)* spirit

umupata *(nom)* gap

umupika *(nom)* pot

umupila *(nom)* ball

umupila *(nom.1)* football

umupina *(nom)* pauper

umupo *(nom)* post

umusalu *(nom.1)* vegetable

umusalu *(nom)* spinach

umusambo *(nom.1)* branch

umushi *(nom)* village

umushili *(nom)* ground

umushishi *(nom)* hair

umusomali *(nom)* nail

umusukupala *(nom)* bottle

umusumba *(nom)* town

umusumba *(act)* state

umusumba *(nom)* community

umusumba umusumba *(nom)* city

umuswaki *(nom.2)* toothbrush

umutemwikwa *(nom)* lover

umutemwikwa *(nom)* beloved

umutende umutende *(nom)* peace

umutenge *(nom.1)* roof

umutengo *(nom)* cost

umuti *(nom)* herb

umuti *(nom)* medicine

umuti wa nshindano *(nom.1)* vaccine

umutiti *(nom)* worm

umuto *(nom)* soup

umuto *(nom)* sauce

umuto *(nom.1)* stew

umutuntula *(adj)* yellow

umutwe *(nom)* head

umwaice *(nom.1)* kid

umwaka upya *(exc)* happy new year

umwakubombela *(nom)* workshop

umwakulila *(nom)* restaurant

umwakupita *(nom)* process

umwakusambila *(nom)* shower

umwana mwaume *(nom)* son

umwana wakubalilapo *(nom)* firstborn

umwana wamfumu umwanakashi *(nom)* princess

umwana wesukulu *(nom)* pupil

umwanakashi *(nom)* lady

umwanakashi *(adj)* female

umwanakashi *(nom)* woman

umwanakashi ushaupwa *(nom)* maiden

umwanda umo *(nom)* century

umwangashi *(nom.1)* wine

umwaume *(adj)* male

umwaume *(nom)* male

umwela *(nom)* wind

umwela *(nom)* air

umwela *(adj)* windy

umwele *(nom)* cutlass

umweni *(nom)* guest

umweni *(nom.1)* foreigner

umwenso *(adj)* nervous

umweo umweo *(nom)* soul

umweo *(adj)* alive

umweshi *(nom.3)* moon

umwikala calo *(nom.1)* citizen

umwina *(nom)* heap

Umwina Afrika *(adj)* African

Umwina America *(nom.1)* American

Umwina Nigeria *(nom.1)* Nigerian

umwina Zambia *(nom)* Zambian

umwine *(nom)* owner

umwine eka *(pro)* herself

umwine wacipe *(nom)* proprietor

umwine wancende *(nom)* landlord

umwinshi *(nom)* gate

umwipi *(nom.1)* dwarf

umwipwa *(nom)* niece

umwishikulu *(nom)* grandchild

umwishikulu *(nom)* granddaughter

umwishikulu *(nom)* grandson

umwishikulu wabashikulu *(nom)* greatgrandchild

yuniversiti university *(nom.0.1)* university

upa *(act)* marry

ushaingila nchito *(adj)* unemployed

utukondo *(nom.3)* toe

utumiti *(nom)* grove

utunyelele *(nom.1)* ants

uwabula mucinshi *(nom)* impertinence

uwakaso *(nom)* miser

uwaku Namibia *(nom)* Namibian

uwaku Zambia *(adj)* Zambian

uwaku Zimbabwe *(nom)* Zimbabwean

uwakulwishanya nankwe *(nom)*
rivalry

uwakutendeka *(nom)* begin-
ner

uwakwafwa *(nom)* assistant

uwakwimininako *(nom.1)* rep-
resentative

uwalubuli *(nom)* bullying

uwamano *(nom)* genius

uwankumbu *(adj)* gracious

uwapulishamo *(nom)* Almighty

uyu *(pro)* he

uyu *(pro)* she

uyu *(det)* this

vacha *(nom)* voucher

vayoleti *(adj)* violet

velanda *(nom)* verandah

vesi vesi *(nom)* verse

vidyo *(nom.1)* video

vodika *(nom)* vodka

volyumu *(nom.1)* volume

vota *(act)* vote

wa *(act)* fall

wa maka yonse *(adj)* almighty

wa misoka *(nom)* murderer

waleyalan *(nom.1)* verb

wama *(adj)* pleasant

wama *(adv)* better

wamina *(nom.1)* advantage

wamya *(adj)* correct

wamya *(act)* clean

wamya *(adj)* clean

wati dɔw la *(adv)* sometimes

weather *(nom.1)* weather

weba *(act)* tell

website *(nom.1)* website

weka *(nom)* self

weka *(adv)* alone

wemwine weka *(pro)* yourself

wesha *(act)* try

whoa *(exc)* whoa

wikala *(act)* sit

wilo *(nom.1)* wheel

wina *(act)* win

wina *(nom)* winner

windo *(nom.0)* window

wisha *(act)* throw away

wiso *(nom.1)* whistle

wita *(act)* call

ya *(act)* go

yaa *(nom)* Yaa

yakwe *(pro)* his

yandi *(pro)* my

ye *(pro)* ye

yemba *(adj)* beautiful

yerusalemu *(din.1)* Jerusalem

Yesu Yesu *(din)* Jesus

yohane *(din.1)* John

Zambia *(nom)* Zambia

zero *(adj)* zero

zimbabwe *(nom)* Zimbabwe

zoo *(nom)* zoo

Zulu *(nom.1)* Zulu

Index

open *isula*, 89
opposite *pusene*, 113
oppression *ukusupikwa*, 127
option *sala*, 114
or *atemwa*, 61
orange *icungwa*, 80
orange *linkolobwe*, 98
order *ka kofɔ*, 90
order *tankile*, 118
organ *ciputulwa camubili*, 70
organism *akabulungwa*, 58
organization *akabungwe*, 58
organizer *kabika*, 90
Oromo *Olomo*, 109
ostentatious *ukuilanga*, 123
other *cimbi*, 69
our *we esu*, 72
our *we*, 14, 34
ours *ifyesu*, 81
ourselves *ifwe fweka*, 81
out *fuma*, 73
outdoors *kunse*, 96
outside *panse*, 111
outskirt *kunse kwa musumba*, 96
oven *icitofu*, 80
overgrow *ka sanbala yɛlɛn*, 90
owe *owe*, 109
owl *cipululu*, 70
owner *umwine*, 133
ox *mutungu*, 105

Pacific *pasifiki*, 111
paddle *nkafi*, 107
padlock *padiloko*, 110

page *bula*, 65
pail *mbeketi*, 101
pain *ukukalipwa*, 124
painful *kalipa*, 92
paint *penta*, 111
palace *ing'anda ya mfumu*, 85
palm *ndupi*, 107
palmnut *kambili*, 92
pan *pani*, 111
Panjabi *Punjabi*, 113
paper *ipepala*, 88
parable *umulumbe*, 130
parched *ica kambatikwa*, 75
parent *ubufyashi*, 120
parent *umufyashi*, 130
parents *abafyashi*, 58
park *paki*, 110
parliament *parliament*, 111
parliamentarian *parliamentarian*, 111
parrot *mucence*, 103
parsley *pasili*, 111
part *iciputulwa*, 79
partner *mwina obe umwina mobe*, 106
party *ukusefya*, 126
pass *pita*, 112
pass by *cilila*, 69
passion *bucushi*, 64
paste *musunga*, 105
pastor *kakumba*, 91
path *inshila*, 86
patience *kushipikisha*, 96

Cisungu kasahorow

bem.kasahorow.org/app/l

- Bemba Family Dictionary: Bemba-English
- My Body in Bemba
- My First Bemba Dictionary
- Concise Bemba
- My First Bemba Counting Book
- Bemba Children's Dictionary
- Modern Bemba Dictionary : Bemba-English and English-Bemba

KWID: G-KKK25-BEM-EN-2022-07-28
www.kasahorow.org/booktalk
Natotela! Thank you!

Printed in Great Britain
by Amazon